MAKING TELECOMMUTING HAPPEN

Larry Press's VNR Titles

- CD ROM: Facilitating Electronic Publishing
  by Linda Helgerson

- The Digital Workplace: Designing Groupware Platforms
  by Charles Grantham

- Computer Augmented Teamwork: A Guided Tour
  by Robert Bostrom

- Broadband Networking
  by Lawrence Gasman

- Executive Information Systems
  by Wayne Burkan

- IBM's Systems Applications Architecture
  by Stephen Randesi and Donald Czubek

- IBM's Systems Network Architecture
  by Stephen Randesi and Donald Czubek

- Introdution to Curves and Surfaces of Computer Design
  by Robert Beach

- New Wave
  by Miles Kehoe

- Voice Communication with Computers
  by Chris Schmandt

- Making Telecommuting Happen
  by Jack Nilles

MAKING TELECOMMUTING HAPPEN

A Guide for Telemanagers and Telecommuters

JACK M. NILLES

VNR

VAN NOSTRAND REINHOLD
New York

Library of Congress Catalog Card Number 94-2061
ISBN 0-442-01857-6

I(T)P Van Nostrand Reinhold is an International Thomson Publishing company.
ITP logo is a trademark under license.

Printed in the United States of America

Van Nostrand Reinhold
115 Fifth Avenue
New York, NY 10003

International Thomson Publishing GmbH
Königswinterer Str. 418
53227 Bonn
Germany

International Thomson Publishing
Berkshire House,168-173
High Holborn, London WC1V 7AA
England

International Thomson Publishing Asia
221 Henderson Bldg. #05-1
Singapore 0315

Thomas Nelson Australia
102 Dodds Street
South Melbourne 3205
Victoria, Australia

International Thomson Publishing Japan
Kyowa Building, 3F
2-2-1 Hirakawacho
Chiyoda-ku, Tokyo 102
Japan

Nelson Canada
1120 Birchmount Road
Scarborough, Ontario
M1K 5G4, Canada

Illustrations by Chris Suddick Neiburger

AFCFF 16   15   14   13   12   11   10 9 8 7 6 5 4 3 2 1

Library of Congress Cataloging-in-Publication Data
Nilles, Jack M.
    Making telecommuting happen / Jack M. Nilles.
              p.   cm.
    Includes index.
    ISBN 0-442-01857-6
    1. Telecommuting—United States.   I. Title.
HD2336.U5N55   1994
331.25—dc20   94-2061
                                    CIP

Contents

Preface

This book is the result of more than twenty years of thinking about and testing telecommuting. After almost two decades of being a "rocket scientist" designing various types of spacecraft for the U.S. government and managing a number of research and development programs, I began to think about ways by which all of that technology could be applied to "the real world." In my education as a physicist with a liberal arts background, as well as my subsequent management assignments, I learned to continually question the fundamentals: *Why are we doing things this way? Why can't we use the technology to do things better?* Two series of events changed the direction of my thinking.

The first was an assignment in 1970 to brief the new Director of NASA on the potential civilian applications of space in the 1980s, a twenty-year forecast for NASA's planning purposes. Many of the interesting applications we postulated had to do with communications satellites. One of them revolved around sending medical information via satellite from the U.S. to Africa in order to help cope with a natural disaster. The satellite was used because it wasn't possible to send the doctors there in time. The experiences with the famine in Ethiopia, the Sudan and Somalia more than twenty years later were an eerie reminder of that scenario.

The second series of events was a set of visits I paid to city planners in 1971. A recurring item in our discussions was the problem of reducing the commuting that was polluting the landscape. Again, the questions kept circulating: Why are we doing things this way? Why not use our technology to make things better? We got around to the possible uses of telecommunications and computers to do the job. The proverbial light bulb went on in my head. An epiphany. This was an incredibly simple and powerful idea, one that could change the world. *Why do we all have to GO to work when technology allows most of us to work at or near home at least some of the time?*

I spent a good part of that year and the next trying to talk my company and the National Science Foundation into supporting some research on what I called the telecommunications-transportation tradeoff. My point was, no matter how brilliant the idea, it had to be reduced to practice—and shown to make good economic sense—in order to be widely accepted. In order to test the concept, my company would have to hire economists, lawyers and psychologists, among others, to make sure that it really worked. No soap. The company wanted to stick strictly to engineering problems, not fool with that fuzzy sociological stuff.

In frustration, I complained one day to one of my colleagues, Dr. Jack Munushian, who had left my company to (among other things) develop an interactive instructional television system at the University of Southern California. At his suggestion I, too, moved to USC in 1972. In 1973 I headed an interdisciplinary research team that received a grant from the National Science Foundation (where the idea apparently had been percolating for a year or two). The objective of the grant was to study federal policy issues on the telecommunications–transportation tradeoff, using a real live company as a test bed.

However, *Development of Policy On the Telecommunications-Transportation Tradeoff,* the grant's title, does not come trippingly off the tongue, so I had to think of a term for this concept that was more direct and intuitive. Telecommuting was the result, followed shortly by teleworking to describe broader applications. The project went swimmingly. In 1974 we published the final report, followed by a book that was published in 1976 in the U.S. and in 1977 in Japan.

In the midst of the project, early in 1974, I had an experience that I have often used to illustrate the motivation for telecommuting. I was driving (alone) from home to the university one morning. As usual, the traffic was start and stop, mostly stop, on the Santa Monica "Free"way. The freeway has a series of large electric signboards located at intervals along its median strip. The purpose of the signboards is to flash traffic advisories to the freeway occupants. That morning there I was, completely stopped, staring at a seemingly endless string of glowing red brakelights ahead of me. I glanced up at the electric signboard ahead. It said: MAINTAIN YOUR SPEED. My speed was zero! And the clock was ticking. I was convinced that telecommuting had a future.

Having demonstrated that telecommuting was economically effective, our team thought that the world would then follow the better mousetrap (or field of dreams) scenario. For several years I tried to encourage various federal agencies to launch further demonstration projects, if only to see if our 1973–74 project was a fluke. None would. The general excuse was: It's not our mission. It was not the mission of the U.S. Department of Transportation because its task was to improve roads, freeways, and mass transit systems, not reduce demand for them. It was not the mission of the U.S. Department of Energy because its job was to increase automobile engine efficiency, not reduce automobile use. It was not the mission of the Environmental Protection Agency, because its job was to reduce automobile pollution, not reduce the number of polluters, and so on. Bureaucratic ring around the rosy.

By 1980 I had given up on the feds. The State of California turned out to be more responsive and, in 1983, the California Energy Commission sponsored our study of the energy impacts of teleworking. That study expanded on the work we had done in 1974 and particularized it to California. Again, the results looked promising but, I felt, needed further testing to see if telecommuting really would work as promised for large numbers of people.

Also, during the late 1970s and early 1980s, a number of companies in the U.S. and Europe tried telecommuting on a small scale. Often, the projects failed, usually because the originators had not thought out and prepared for the management issues. The most important of the management issues was the reluctance of managers to change their methods of management. Some of the projects that were successful died later because the intrapreneurs who sparked them were promoted out of the program before they had reached critical mass. The continuing successes tended to go underground; the companies wouldn't talk about them. Their shyness was easily explained: Why tell your competitors that you have a method of increasing productivity by more than 10%—while actually reducing costs— that doesn't require much of an investment?

This situation convinced me that telecommuting needed some more demonstration projects that were both public, in that the results would be made available, and quantitative—they had to show the bottom-line impacts.

In the mid-1980s, I was able to assemble a group of Fortune 100 companies, to support and participate in a project at the Center for Futures Research at USC, that would make another extended test of telecommuting. The results were similar to those of a decade earlier. Telecommuting still worked and the primary barriers to it were still the attitudes and training of managers. Technology was not a particular problem.

The 1983 Energy Commission project instigated a request by the state of California to plan a telecommuting demonstration project. We completed that in 1985, with a number of state agencies participating in the plan development. In 1987, the state decided to go ahead with a multi-agency, multi-year demonstration project involving more than 230 telecommuters. By 1990 it, too, was a success.[1] The governor established telecommuting as a mandatory option to be considered by every state agency, both as a means of travel reduction and for disaster preparedness. The Loma Prieta earthquake of 1989 may have had an influence on that decision; several telecommuters from the California Public Utilities Commission were able to keep right on working from home, even though its office building in downtown San Francisco was closed for post-quake cleanup and repairs.

During all this period, the global forces toward telecommuting were strengthening: the population was growing; air pollution was getting worse; the daily commute was getting worse; young families were being forced to move farther away from their employers in order to find affordable housing; political instability in the Middle East continued; energy conservation was still an issue; the other ways of reducing car use for commuting—ride-sharing and increased mass transit use—weren't having enough impact.

And the word was getting around. Millions of U.S. information workers were becoming *teleguerillas*, inventing telecommuting for themselves and somehow convincing their supervisors to let them work at home part of the time. The Southern California Association of Governments ran a small internal test of telecommuting. California's South Coast Air

---

[1] Copies of our final report on the project may still be available from the State of California. Write to Forms and Publications; Department of General Services; P.O. Box 1015, North Highlands; Sacramento, CA 95660 for Stock No. 7540-930-1400-0.

Quality Management District issued Regulation XV, a requirement that employers with at least 100 employees reporting to a specific site in the area require ride-sharing, telecommuting or some other way of reducing the number of cars coming into the parking lot—or pay a stiff fine. The Washington State Energy Office initiated a public–private-sector multi-year demonstration of telecommuting in the Puget Sound area. Both the city and county of Los Angeles began telecommuting programs for their employees; the county as an operational reality, the city as a demonstration program. The Federal Government began its Flexiplace program. In 1992 the European-Community-sponsored European Community Telework Forum began a continuing series of seminars around Europe to inform government and business of the advantages of teleworking. In 1993, the EC funded an initiative to demonstrate telecommuting in four major European cities. The state of California started its Telecenters program to establish a set of neighborhood telework centers throughout the state. On January 17, 1994, a major earthquake in the Los Angeles area caused a massive reawakening to the potential of telecommuting at all levels of government and business.

Ever since we formalized our telecommuting training manuals in the mid-1980s we have been asked to release them to the public. With all of the growing interest in telecommuting, it is clear that there is a need for basic how-to instruction. This book is a compilation and expansion of those manuals. I hope that it fills the bill.

Acknowledgments

An enormous number of people contributed to this book in one way or another. Among the first were the regional planners who goaded me into rethinking the problems of transportation congestion; Zohrab Kaprielian and Jack Munushian of USC, who talked me into jumping from outer space to the earth's surface; and my colleagues at The Aerospace Corporation whom I was able to infect with enthusiasm about this crazy idea in 1970. The research faculty team at USC, particularly Paul Gray, Rick Carlson and Gerry Hanneman, were major contributors to that first proof-of-concept project in 1973. Paul Gray has continued his contributions to telecommuting since then. Rich Harkness of Boeing, Peter Goldmark of CBS Laboratories, Alex Reid of University College in London, Joe Coates of the National Science Foundation, Quincy Jones (the architect) and Murray Turoff of the New Jersey Institute of Technology also helped crystallize my thinking in those early days.

Burt Nanus and Sel Enzer of USC's Center for Futures Research, and Warren Bennis of the Graduate School of Business Administration at USC have given me moral support and contributed their special insights for years. Monty Mohrman and Omar El Sawy of USC were instrumental in honing some evaluation concepts for telecommuting. Rick Higgins of Pacific Bell, Frank Miller of IBM, Dennis Acebo of GTE, and Donna Stubbs of Honeywell were important players in making telecommuting happen in the mid 1980s. Those projects helped prompt my development of telecommuting training manuals.

Gil Gordon and Joanne Pratt helped refine the training concepts and commented on the versions of the manuals used in the California Telecommuting Pilot Project. David Fleming was a major force in making telecommuting happen in California government. He and his collaborator, Lis, also contributed their senses of humor at stressful points—it isn't always easy to make telecommuting happen. David has continued his dedication to telecommuting in the California Neighborhood Telecenters Program. Susan Herman and Wally Siembab served in similar roles for the Los Angeles project. Wally has continued to contribute his insights since the official end of that project. He has added further anecdotes from his role in the Telecommunications for Clean Air program.

Hundreds of telecommuters and telemanagers have been given previous versions of much of this material over the past decade. They are the people who ultimately had to make telecommuting happen in the real world. They have done a great job of it. Their comments have instigated a number of additions and revisions to the various versions of the manuals.

Chris Suddick Neiburger has added her inimitable sense of humor—sharpened by personal telecommuting experience—to help humanize what could easily become a very dry topic. A cogent validation of her skill was when one of our telecommuter trainees pointed to the cartoon that is now the lead-in to Part Two and said: *"That's me!"*

The editorial staff at Van Nostrand Reinhold did a masterful job of accelerating the production schedule in its final stages. Special thanks to Dianne Littwin, Chris Grisonich, Risa Cohen, Elizabeth Gehrman, Ellen Reavis, and Elyse Strongin for their quick response times and excellent advice.

A constant source of inspiration and motivation has been my wife and partner, Laila (the LA of JALA). Without her help, understanding, participation and encouragement, this book (as well as some others) might not have been written.

A major problem with writing acknowledgments is that someone is always left out in the heat of final delivery deadlines. For that I apologize in advance. I am writing this between earthquake aftershocks so, in the excitement, I may have missed some important contributors.

Jack M. Nilles
Los Angeles

Introduction and Overview

Teleworking: ANY form of substitution of information technologies (such as telecommunications and computers) for work-related travel.

Telecommuting:[1] *moving the work to the workers instead of moving the workers to work; periodic work out of the central office, one or more days per week either at home or in a telework center.*

This is a guide to what seems to many to be a new kind of work situation: telecommuting. As with most new situations, it presents both opportunities and risks. Telecommuting, as defined above, emphasizes reducing or eliminating that daily commute to work for employees (or owners) of an organization. Our tests over the past two decades have shown that, for most organizations, managers and telecommuters, the opportunities of telecommuting far outweigh the risks. The key to making the best use of these opportunities is proper planning and the development of an appropriate management style. Management style is one of the main subjects of this book.

The book is designed to be a ready reference to you as—and after—you embark upon a rewarding experience as a manager of telecommuters, a telecommuter, or both. The book is divided into two parts. Part One, by far the longest, focuses on general management issues, management policy, including site location, the rules of telecommuting, technology requirements, and costs

---

[1] More formally, the partial or total substitution of telecommunications technologies, possibly with the aid of computers, for the commute to work.

and benefits. It should be read by all managers and by would-be telecommuters who want to learn more about those issues. Part Two concentrates on the specific aspects of setting up and operating a home office. However, this is not a book on starting or operating a home-based business; rather, it is intended for people who now have a principal office somewhere else than at home.

There are ten other chapters. Chapter 1 describes telecommuting, the arguments for and against it, and its various options. Chapters 2 and 3 explore the issues of selecting people who are likely to be good telecommuters and finding or making the proper workplaces for effective telecommuting. Chapters 1 and 2 are mostly review material if you already have been selected as a telemanager.

Chapter 4 explores both today's and future technology needs as telecommuting grows. Its fundamental message is that contemporary, readily available levels of technology are perfectly adequate for large quantities of telecommuting. Chapter 5 gets at that central, often unspoken managerial fear of telecommuting: the threat of losing control. If you don't read anything else in this book, read Chapter 5. It contains a revolutionary central theme: *leaders, not administrators, are what make telecommuting work well.* Leadership *can* be taught. A good leader of telecommuters is a good manager in general. Poor leadership and telecommuting disasters seem to be inseparable. Aside from those philosophical issues, Chapter 5 treats the key procedures for successfully managing telecommuters.

Chapter 7 discusses some of the formalities of telecommuting—rules and regulations—both from the management point of view and the externally imposed ones. such as union rules and zoning laws. This is the chapter that usually gets reworked by the corporate legal staff and/or union representatives. It is very important to study this chapter, discuss it with senior management—and the legal staff—and make any necessary revisions, *before* formal telecommuting begins. Chapter 6 continues that line of thought, concentrating on training workers to cope in different telecommuting situations.

Finally, Chapter 8 gets down to the bottom line. Regardless of how warm and fuzzy telecommuting makes everyone feel, we live in a world where economic competitiveness and survival are real and daily issues. Chapter 8 reviews these matters from all sides: the employer, the telecommuter, and the community. However, the emphasis is on the employer's point of view because that's who makes the critical decision to allow or encourage telecommuting.

Part Two starts with Chapter 9, although every telecommuter should also read Chapters 3 and 7. Chapter 9 concentrates on the details of setting up a home office. Chapter 10 gets at the practical aspects of peaceful coexistence with the other members of your household, your neighbors, and your boss and colleagues.

Finally, there is a set of appendices that provide sample forms for various aspects of the mutual employer-employee agreement on the terms of telecommuting. This, too, should be scoured by your legal staff before formal telecommuting begins.

This book is a variant of the one we have been using since the mid-1980s for Fortune 100 companies and large government and/or public sector organizations. Although I often use the term *company* in what follows, please take that to mean your own organization, of whatever size.

The book is written under the presumption that your company will want to test (we prefer *demonstrate*) telecommuting with a selected sample of the staff before making it generally available to all eligible employees. Therefore, in many places the book discusses telecommuting in terms of the "Company Demonstration Project." After a demonstration project of suitable duration (say, at least one year) is complete, then more permanent rules can be written that apply to your firm, based on that experience.

PART
1

MOSTLY FOR MANAGERS
(Telecommuters Should Peek)

1

Concepts of Telecommuting

Principles of Decentralization

Telecommuting is a form of *decentralized* work. Since the industrial revolution started early in the 19th century the trend in industrializing countries has been to *centralize* workplaces. The reason is simple: industries, factories and assembly plants, needed centralization. To run efficiently, they needed to be located near sources of materials, supplies, and production workers: cities and their transportation hubs. As industries grew, so did the cities in which they were located. As new forms of transportation developed it was possible to make ever bigger cities, with ever bigger industries hiring ever bigger and more concentrated workforces. Everything was at hand to the industrial manager: the raw materials brought by train or truck, the processing machines, and the industrial workers. This model of the world pervades our society, even in businesses and government organizations that have nothing to do with manufacturing.

We don't think twice about it. In order to work you must *go* to work. Just like all the other factory workers.

Well, Rip, while you were asleep the world changed.

Why Decentralize?

Since the mid-1950s manufacturing has been steadily declining as a source of employment. In 1990 fewer than 1 in 3.7 U.S. workers were in manufacturing or repair trades; fewer than 1 in

1

54 U.S. workers were on farms, according to the Bureau of the Census. On the other hand, 57% or more of the U.S. workforce comprises information or knowledge workers, whose jobs derive from their creation, collation, manipulation, transformation, and/or dissemination of information or from their operation of information machines such as typewriters and computers. Figure 1-1 tells the story: Most work now and in the foreseeable future will be information work.

Figure 1-1 *Historical and future workforce composition*

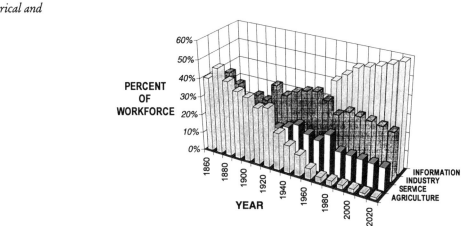

Source: Porat "The Information Economy", JALA forecasts

Increasingly these information workers are using telephones, computers, or telecommunications-connected computers to do their work. They are moving their work around, instead of themselves.

Here are some situations where the traditional ways of doing things—centralized work in the information factory—is not only old hat but is counterproductive. Score your own organization on these.

• The commute to (and from) work is more than normally dangerous and/or takes more than *forty* minutes a day *round trip* (for at least half your employees), and during that commute you and/or your employees are not doing something either pleasurable or useful. See Figure 1-2 for a view of what commuting costs you in terms of waking days per year (that is, sixteen-hour days—I assume that you sleep about eight hours per day, but not while you're commuting). Multiply that by every one of your commuters. This one is worth 20 points.

- The perils of commuting chronically create late arrivals and early departures among your employees, with adjustment to- or from-work periods immediately adjacent thereto. Minor complaints, problems with the kids and routine dental or medical appointments turn into sick days off. Productivity is sliding. This, too, gets 20 points.
- There are too many meetings that are insufficiently focused and wander off into time-wasting, irrelevant topics. Time management is a growing problem. At least 15 points for this. You get 25 points if you attend more than ten meetings per week.

Figure 1-2 *Commuting as a time-waster*

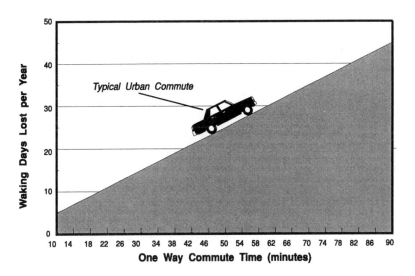

- The working environment produces high levels of stress and productivity loss because of those crucial *Three I's*: interruptions, interruptions, and interruptions. This nets 15 points. Minimum.
- You are running out of office space—or rental costs have gotten out of hand. Overcrowding is having serious effects on morale and productivity. Another 15 points here.
- You're having trouble attracting or retaining *skilled* employees. 15 points for this; make it 20 points if your annual turnover rate for skilled workers is higher than 10%.
- Air pollution in your area is getting worse. A good part of it is because of all those commuter cars on the roads. Another

15 points for this, 25 points if you're in an area that has strict regional air pollution regulations.

This is by no means an exhaustive list, but it delivers the message: physical centralization brings a variety of problems in urban environments. Big cities, in particular, impose growing costs on everyone who works within them. If your score on this list was above 75, centralization is seriously eroding your organization's performance. A score between 50 and 75 shows significant damage and even 15 points or more should cause you to consider whether there might not be a better way than what most organizations have been doing for the past twenty years. Please note that some of the situations just described (such as meetingitis) are not confined to centralized organizations, but sometimes decentralization helps. Also note that centralization can be just as bad—even worse—in the suburbs as in central cities. Just because your company relocated to the boonies, it doesn't get you off the hook. You may also want to change the weighting of some or all of the questions to better suit your organization's priorities. Do so, then test the situation again.

Having Your Cake and Eating It Too

The industrial motive for centralization—efficient concentration of resources—was vital for effective industrial development. That concentration of resources, that accessibility to the raw materials and tools you need to do the job is equally vital in information work. If you are an information worker you need to have the information necessary for your job; you need to have that information when *you* need it and in the form best suited for your requirements—or at least moldable by your information tools. You and your employees need to be the foci of information flows. Well, of course. That stands to reason. No doubt about it. *[Add your own favorite cliché here.]* Everybody needs centralization!

But suppose you and your employees could get all of this information *without* commuting more than forty minutes (round trip) per day, eroding working time, failing to meet scheduling challenges, getting stressed out, losing key people, violating air pollution regulations, and otherwise debilitating the organization. Suppose that you could keep that form of *logical* centralization—continuous access to the information you need to do the job—without the *physical* centralization characteristic of an industrial society.

Well, it's possible. You can keep connected *logically* while decentralizing *physically*. You *can* keep many of your means of production accessible without clumping them together in the same place. You *can* keep your heads together without having to keep your bodies together. You *can* move the work to the worker instead of moving the worker to the work. You and/or your employees *can* telecommute.

How Is It Possible?   The reason you can telecommute is that information technology has developed to the point where the necessary information can get to us no matter where or when we are. Our jobs, for some of us, have become *location-independent*. The number of people who fit this category is increasing daily. You probably already have a number of telecommuters in your organization, covert though they may be. There's more on this in Chapter 4 but here is an overview.

Telecommunications

In the last few years telecommunications technology has made significant advances. Electronic switching and fiber optics have multiplied both the speed and volume of telephone circuits where they have been installed. Fiber optics have become so capable that they are replacing satellite circuits for many long-distance communication paths.

The telephone network is going digital all over the world. This means that it is becoming easier and more reliable for computers to talk to each other over the phone lines. This digital switching and communications technology also allows a number of new services to be provided to business and residential customers. Call forwarding, call waiting, caller identification, call blocking, auto dialing, voice mail, electronic banking, telephone-, computer-, and video-teleconferencing, videotex, and more are becoming ubiquitous. Cellular telephones add mobility as well as versatility for the individual telecommunications user. LANs, WANs, ISDN, and ATM[1] are the acronyms of instant electronic togetherness.

---

[1] Local Area Networks, Wide Area Networks, Integrated Services Digital Networks, and Asynchronous Transfer Modes are methods of sending information around the building or the world in digital—computer

Many kinds of information work may need only one or a few of these telecommunications services to make telecommuting viable. But each new technology addition—and each new reduction in cost for the existing technology—opens the way for more telecommuting and more telecommuters.

Computers

Computers, particularly microcomputers, add an entirely new range and intensity of colors to the telecommuting palette. Personal computers suitable for most routine business functions: text and document processing, spreadsheets, graphics, data banks, and the like, are available for less than what an electric typewriter used to cost a few years ago. We expect that, well before the year 2000, most office desks in the U.S. will have computers on or very close to them. Most of those computers will be connected (ultimately, if not at first) to some form of telecommunications, probably a telephone line or a local area network (which in turn will be connected to one or more telephone lines or satellite circuits). Furthermore, the capabilities of the computers, per dollar invested in new hardware, are increasing every year; by a factor of ten about every seven years.

At present it is quite feasible to have a home-based office that has greater information processing capability than the "Principal" (that is, main/headquarters) office, if the principal office has not kept up with technological advances. This book was produced in a home-based office. As you see it. A product of telecommuting.

Forms of Telecommuting

There will be more on the technology later. For now, rest assured that there are few technological barriers today for effective telecommuting. The biggest barriers are right behind our eyes. But before we look at those, let's examine the different flavors of telecommuting. There are two main variants: home-based and telework center telecommuting. And then there are variants of those variants, to suit your needs.

---

understandable—form. Although LANs aren't strictly telephone-based, they are often connected to the telephone system.

**Chocolate—
Home-Based
Telecommuting**

Everyone loves chocolate. The press particularly love home-based telecommuting. It's such a startling departure from *Work As We Know It*. It immediately captures the imagination: work in idyllic surroundings at home instead of some miserable, stuffy, noisy old office. Work at your own pace, neither pushed nor impeded by your fellow workers. Fit your work life into your family life instead of *vice versa*. Design your own job. Dramatically increase your productivity—and your job opportunities.

Sounds too good to be true, doesn't it?

For some people it *is* true *all* of the time. For many, many others, *some* of it is true *all* of the time. For still more, *some* of it is true *some* of the time. For still others, none of it is true. Part of what we do in the next chapter is to sort these options out.

The basic idea of home-based telecommuting is this:

Home can be an effective base for telecommuting, allowing significant cost reductions for both employer and employee, allowing employees access to jobs that otherwise might not be available, allowing employers access to people who otherwise would not be available, providing significant productivity gains and a host of indirect benefits to society (energy conservation, pollution reduction, etc.). The air pollution reduction aspect of this is a major incentive for many organizations to be involved in telecommuting, generally in response to increasingly strict environmental regulations. *For most employees, home-based telecommuting works only as a part-time option.*

Home-based telecommuters should have a well-defined area within their homes that is treated as office space. Within that space is all the equipment and supplies that are needed for their job.

In 1993, most U.S. telecommuters were home-based, telecommuting only part of the time, according to our own estimates and those of a number of other sources. Estimates of the number of U.S. telecommuters in 1993 ranged from about 3 million (our estimate) to more than 20 million (an estimate presumably including *all* work-at-home people, most of whom are not telecommuters). About 600,000 telecommuters were in Southern California alone (*before* the 1994 earthquakes).

Vanilla—Satellite Telework Centers

A satellite telework center may seem much less glamorous than home-based telecommuting. A satellite telework center is an office building, or part of a building, that is wholly owned (or leased) by an organization, to which its employees regularly report for work. It looks much like any other set of offices—with some individual cubicles of various sizes, desks, computers, telephones, conference rooms, and so on—although the mixture of these may be different from a more conventional office.

There is one important difference between a satellite office and a traditional office: *All of the center's employees work there because they live closer to that facility than to their regular or principal office, regardless of what their jobs are.* That is, for an organization with several satellite telework centers (or field/branch offices), its telecommuting accountants may be scattered physically among a few or all of the satellites, rather than at a single location to which they all report. The interconnectedness of the Accounting Department comes through telecommunications, not through collocation. Of course, as in home-based telecommuting, many, if not most, satellite office telecommuters also telecommute only part-time.

Satellite telework centers can save significant amounts of commuting while still providing environments like those of traditional offices. They also can take advantage of lower costs per square foot of the office space they do use, because of their suburban, small town, or redeveloping central city locations. The main disadvantage of satellite centers is that they require a certain amount of facilities planning and administration to operate effectively. Further, if employees mostly still drive their cars to the centers, the air pollution improvements may be diminished significantly.[2]

---

[2] For example, the South Coast Air Quality Management District in Southern California does not count telecommuting to a telework center as the equivalent of eliminating a commute to work unless the one-way commute has been reduced by at least 20 miles.

Chocolate Chip—Local Telework Centers

A local telework center is almost the same as a satellite center. The difference here is that the building may house employees from several different organizations. Otherwise, each organization's set of offices are arranged as if it were a satellite center.

Some of the additional advantages of local telework centers are: the ability to share services (telecommunications, large computers, cafeterias, environmental control, etc.); the ability to have more, smaller, distributed offices; relief from building ownership worries. Disadvantages, compared with satellite telework centers, seem to concentrate on less control over office space, including physical security.

Some local telework centers are *really* local, serving a neighborhood. Naturally enough, they are called *neighborhood* telework centers. As you might expect, neighborhood centers tend to support only a few telecommuters, generally fewer than 20. The emphasis in neighborhood centers is to eliminate car use in getting to and from the center. Telecommuters either walk there from home, bicycle or take mass transit. In 1994 the State of California, in its TeleCenters project, began testing several different versions of neighborhood centers scattered throughout the state. Often, particularly in Europe, they are located in rural areas, towns, and villages, and combined with other types of businesses, such as retail stores and business services, in the same building.

Tutti Frutti—Combinations

These four (three-and-a-half, really) flavors of telecommuting can be combined and mixed as appropriate for any given organization. For example, most home-based telecommuters will work part-time at home, the rest of the time in their principal office, a satellite, or a local telework center. A few home telecommuters will still go to the office most days, but will telecommute at both ends of the work day, going to and from the office during off-peak traffic hours. (This is OK for cutting commuting time but doesn't have much of an impact on reducing air pollution.) Satellite and local centers in well-designed operations are likely to have both permanent office space for their full-time employees and temporary spaces both for their home or occasional telecommuters and for employees from other cities who need temporary space during a trip.

The central criterion for telecommuting is the same for all of these:

If a job, or major portions of it, does not intrinsically depend on the location of the worker, then it is *telecommutable*. The issue then becomes one of who, when, where, and how, not whether.

The issue of who and when comes in the next chapter.

But Does It Pay?

Unquestionably. Our own experience and that of others shows a number of benefits of successful telecommuting, benefits for employers, employees and the community at large. These benefits include:

- Significantly increased productivity
- Reduced turnover rates (and related new employee recruitment and training costs)
- Reduced office space requirements
- Lowered real estate costs
- Better management
- Increased organizational flexibility
- Faster response times
- Increased employee morale
- A cleaner environment
- Reduced energy consumption and diminished dependence on fossil fuels
- Greater participation by telecommuters in local activities

This is what you can expect to get from *successful* telecommuting. Our experience has been that new telecommuting programs, even including all the costs of planning, design, organization, technology change, training and management innovation, will pay for themselves in a year or less.

Unfortunately, as in so many other areas of life, it is distinctly possible to have *unsuccessful* telecommuting. There are many ways to do it wrong, several of which have already been tried and proven by large organizations. In an unsuccessful telecommuting program the reverse of the list above can occur.

Which is why this book exists. There are a few key principles to making telecommuting work. None of these principles is particularly difficult or revolutionary; they are simply good management practices. But they are more important, perhaps, in telecommuting than in ordinary management situations. Here they are:

- Pick your telecommuters carefully;
- Set up the proper working environments and technology and telecommunications support;
- Jointly establish performance-oriented evaluation procedures;
- Train the telecommuters, their co-workers, and (as appropriate) their families;
- Get frequent feedback on how well you're doing, and
- Alter your procedures and rules, as appropriate, in response to the feedback.

Telecommuting vs. Teleworking

Most of the preceding discussion—and most of this book—concentrates on telecommuting, the substitution of information technology for the commute to and from work, as defined in the beginning of the first chapter. But most of the material in this book also applies to teleworking as well. The two are related as shown in Figure 1-3.

Telecommuting is a form of teleworking. In fact, if you stretch the commute distance to a few hundred miles, or whatever distance precludes frequent commuting, you have teleworking. Teleworking also includes your everyday travel substitution that occurs while you're in your principal office—after you have commuted to work. Almost everyone is a teleworker at least some of the time.

In Europe, the situation is somewhat more confusing. Several European languages have no word for commuting,[3] so telecommuting is lumped together with other forms of telesubstitution under teleworking. Whatever you call it, the operating principles are the same.

The importance of teleworking and telecommuting is a question of degree. A little telecommuting/teleworking may not make an enormous difference to you, your company or your country. But as the amount of telesubstitution increases, so do the options for organizational design and effectiveness, life-style, family and other social relationships, even the shape and nature of villages, towns and cities. Teleworking and its telecommuting components provide tools for change that, properly used, can have positive effects on all of these.

The following chapters address the nature and uses of those tools. By following them, you can enhance your chances of developing and maintaining an effective telecommuting or teleworking operation.

Figure 1-3 *The Relationship Between Telecommuting and Teleworking.*

---

[3] In 1992 the French coined a term for telecommuting: *télépendulaire*. Loosely translated, it means going back and forth, pendulum-like, at a distance. As of this writing, there is no comparable term in German, Spanish, Italian or any of the scandinavian or Finno-Ugric languages.

Selecting Telecommuters

Over the years we have developed a feel for what it takes to make telecommuting work—a feel backed up by two decades of empirical data. It is possible, we believe, to estimate, before the fact, the likely success of a potential telecommuting situation. The first step is picking the telecommuters themselves. This is done in two stages. The first stage relates to the nature of the job that is to be done. Some jobs are simply not good candidates for one or the other—or any—forms of telecommuting. Some jobs are ideal for telecommuting. Similarly, some job incumbents are perfectly suited for telecommuting, others would be unhappy in some or all telecommuting situations.

Thus there are two parts to the telecommuter selection process. The first part consists of an examination of the content of a potential telecommuter's job. The second part, of most importance to home telecommuters, is an evaluation of the psychological/behavioral aspects of the job and of the potential telecommuters.

Dissecting Jobs

It is easy to see that some jobs are perfect for telecommuting and others are terrible candidates. An author is likely to be a good telecommuter, a bus driver wouldn't work out at all as a telecommuter. But what about those thousands of jobs that are in the middle somewhere? The way to decide whether a job can be telecommuted is to analyze its requirements.

Jobs As Collections of Tasks

Each job—yours, mine, everyone else's—can be viewed as a collection of tasks that must be performed. Tasks are such things as writing reports, analyzing figures, collecting information, providing information, developing plans, coordinating activities of others, digging ditches, painting the house, making coffee. Any job can be analyzed this way. Table 2-1 shows three different, if nameless, information jobs broken down into tasks to be performed.

Table 2-1: TASK BREAKDOWNS FOR SOME INFORMATION JOBS

JOBS AS COLLECTIONS OF TASKS

Tasks for Job:	A	B	C
Preparing reports	5%	10%	
Analyzing figures	15%	5%	10%
Collating information	5%		10%
Providing information	5%	5%	10%
Developing plans	20%	5%	
Interacting with the public	10%	20%	10%
Coordinating information	5%	15%	
Presenting information	10%	15%	
Composing letters and memos	5%	10%	25%
Copying information	5%		15%
Retrieving information	10%		20%
Supervising employees	5%	15%	

To test this, try it on your own job. Make a list, not too detailed, of the tasks you have to perform to satisfy the requirements of your job. A dozen or so tasks should cover most of what you do. Table 2-2 provides some space to try it on.

Make sure that you consider your job over a period of time such as a week, or even several weeks or months, to take into account the fact that most jobs vary their structure from day to day. The task of preparing a report, for example, may take several straight days at a time, but averaged over a period of a few months, report preparation may be only 5% of the work time.

If you don't like to think in percentages, try fractions. The point here is that we want to get an estimate that is quantitative enough so that you'll have a good idea of the job structure.

Table 2-2: TASK BREAKDOWN WORKSHEET

JOBS AS COLLECTIONS OF TASKS		
TASKS FOR:	MY JOB	____'s JOB	____'s JOB
TOTAL	100%	100%	100%

The Simplified Selection Version

If you're a supervisor or manager, do the same thing for some of your employees. Just one or two of them for now, to get an idea of how the pieces of each job fit together: preparing reports, communicating with the public, clients, or co-workers, getting information, performing analyses, whatever.

The main question is: How well can you (or they) do some or all of these tasks from home (assuming you have the necessary equipment and files to do it) and how much of the job needs to be done in the (or an) office? Chances are that there's some of each; that you might be able to work at home part of the time, but there's also a need to be in the office part of the time, too. Estimate how much of the time you *don't* have to be in the office to do each task.

You can rate your job with the assistance of Table 2-3. Here's the procedure.

1. First, let's concentrate on the *Importance to Job* column in Table 2-3. Think about how much time you spend communicating with other people. The first three items deal with the amount of time you spend communicating personally with others, either face-to-face or otherwise (over the telephone, by fax, e-mail, etc.). Note that we are concerned with what is *necessary* for the job. This may not be the way it is done today. For example, the first item deals with the *need* for daily face-to-face contact. You may have a job in which you ordinarily have daily face-to-face contact

Table 2-3: GENERAL JOB TASK ANALYSIS

Nature of Tasks	Importance to Job	Suitability for Work At:			
		Traditional Office Only	*Telework Center*	*Part-Time Home*	*Full-Time Home*
High level of face-to-face daily interaction with others	_____	Best solution	Depends on location of others	Poor	No
Large amount of face-to-face interaction but may be clumped in time	_____	Excellent	Excellent	Good to Excellent	Fair to Poor
High level of interpersonal contac but via telecommunications	_____	Excellent	Excellent	Excellent	Good to Excellent
Fragmented tasks, many "fire drills" requiring coordination	_____	Good to Excellent	Good to Excellent	Fair to Good	Fair to Poor
Fragmented tasks, but often requiring high concentration	_____	Poor	Good to Fair	Good to Excellent	Good to Excellent
Requiring extended concentration, medium to long duration	_____	Poor	Poor to Good	Excellent	Excellent
Need physical access to special, fixed resources	_____	Excellent	Excellent (possibly)	Good if access can be clumped	Poor
Involves sensitive information requiring physical security	_____	Excellent	Good to Excellent	Good to Poor	Poor
Involves sensitive information that can be protected readily (e.g., by encryption)	_____	Excellent	Excellent	Excellent to Good	Excellent to Good
Totals					

with others most of the time but there are many occasions when you could substitute telephone calls for some, if not all, of the contacts.

The total of your answers for these three items should equal one-tenth of the portion of your time you spend in such communication.

For example, let's say you spend 16 hours[1] communicating during an average 40-hour week; that's 40% of your time (16/40ths of the week), so the first 3 entries under Importance to Job should add up to 4 (or one-tenth of 40%). If all of that time is spent in meetings or other face-to-face conversation, then the first two entries should add up to 4 and the third entry should be 0. If, on the other hand, all your communicating time is on the phone, then the first two entries should be 0 and the third should be 4. Most people have a number in each of the spaces. The trick for telecommuting is to work for a 0 in the first entry: zero daily face-to-face meetings. (After this an IRS Form 1040 should be easy!) Don't forget that we're asking about the way you spend your time over a long period, weeks or months. So average these activities over that kind of period.

2. Next, take each of the remaining items in the *Importance to Job* column, decide how well it describes the *average requirements* of your (or your employee's) job, on a scale from 0 to 10, where *0* means it *does not apply* to your job and *10* means it applies completely, *all* of the time.

3. Then, look at each of the rows in the table in turn, and add up the points for each column under *Suitability for Work At*. Our ratings are given for each item under *Suitability for Work At:* for the traditional office, telework office, etc. Score 5 points for each Excellent (or Best Solution), 4 for Very Good, 3 for Good (or OK), 2 for Fair, 1 for Poor, and 0 for No. Multiply each rating by your assessment of the requirement level of the job (the number in the Importance to Job column, then add all nine ratings to get the column total.

For example, to continue the face-to-face case, a job importance rating of 2 would work out to a score of 10 for the traditional office (Best Solution, or 5 × 2); some number between 10 (5 × 2) and 0 (0 × 2) for the telework center (10 if you could still have all the meetings at the center, 0 if you couldn't have any); 2 for part-time home telecommuting

---

[1] On average, telecommuters spend about 14 hours per week communicating.

(Poor, or 1 × 2); and 0 for full-time home telecommuting. Do this scoring for each row and each of the Suitability columns. Now add up all the columns to get a preliminary total score.

And the answer is—whichever column has the highest number of points is the one most suited for that job. For some jobs it's still the traditional office only. For many jobs another column will rate higher. Please note that there is no absolute answer; most jobs can be fitted into several categories with acceptable results.

Now there's one other thing to keep in mind. For this table, make sure you think *only* of the work and communication requirements of the job. Try to divorce those from the personalities involved in your real job, as if you were filling out a job description for someone else in a different department.

A Slightly More Complicated Version

If you want to explore these issues in more detail, try the following. Use Table 2-4 as an example. If you're into computers, set up the list of tasks as column A of a spreadsheet. Head the column "Tasks for the job of <your job title>." If computers are not an intimate part of your life, make the list on a piece of paper.

Down the left-hand column (Column A in the spreadsheet), write out a list of the tasks required to fulfill the requirements of your job. Table 2-4 gives some typical examples. If those don't match your job, enter ones that do. Make sure that everything you are required to do in your job is covered by one of the task items. Keep in mind that these are generic kinds of tasks, analyzing figures, for example, that describe certain kinds of activity.

Label the next column (Column B in the spreadsheet): "Percent of Job." As in the previous analysis, think about how you spend your time over a period of several days to several months; in any case, long enough so that you have spent time doing all of the tasks listed in the first column. If you keep a desk calendar, maybe it would help to refer to it. Now, estimate what percent of that total time you spend doing each of the listed tasks. For example, in Table 2-4 the holder of Job B spends 15% of her time coordinating information and 0% collating information.

If you're a current or potential supervisor of telecommuters, you might want to do the same thing for some of your colleagues or people who work for you. Just one or two of them for now, to get an idea of how the pieces of each job fit together.

Now comes an important part. Make another column (Column C). Label it "Location-Dependent Percent of Task."

What we're looking for here is a number that summarizes the fraction of time that specifically depends on the location of the person who performs the task. This number is composed of three elements. To keep Table 2-4 less daunting, we show only the one column; but think of each entry as composed of three elements:

- The face-to-face requirement
- Dependencies on specific, fixed locations
- Dependencies on alternate or variable locations

Table 2-4: ANALYSIS OF JOB B

Task	% of the Job	Location DEpen-dent % of TASK	Location Depen-dence as % of JOB	Location INdepen-dence
Preparing reports	10	10	1	9
Analyzing figures	5	0	0	5
Collating information	0	0	0	0
Providing information	5	60	3	2
Developing plans	5	20	1	4
Interacting with clients or public	20	40	8	12
Coordinating information	15	20	3	12
Presenting information	15	100	15	0
Composing letters and/or memos	10	0	0	10
Copying information	0	0	0	0
Retrieving information	0	0	0	0
Supervising others	10	20	2	8
Keeping current	5	0	0	5
TOTAL LOCATION INDEPENDENCE				67
REALITY FACTOR (average in-office days/week)				3
AVERAGE PRACTICAL INDEPENDENCE[2] **(potential home telecommuting days/wk)**				2

---

[2] Assuming a five-day week. For compressed or other modified work schedules, subtract the number after Reality Factor from the average total work days per week to the final answer.

Separating Face-to-Face and Other Location-Dependent Tasks From the Rest

Face-to-Face Tasks. First, for each task, decide how much of its successful performance *requires* that there be *face-to-face* interaction between the performer of the task and other people. The *requires* part of this is important. If interpersonal interaction is needed to do the task, but that interaction can be accomplished over the telephone or by electronic mail or teleconferencing, or even interoffice memo, then face-to-face interaction is not required for the task.

For some parts of your task list, this is a simple problem. If you need to write a report, but only need written reference materials to do it, you have those materials at hand and you're doing the writing on a personal computer, then it is likely that you can put 0% as the percentage of face-to-face interaction required for that task. If the task depends entirely on interacting with others face-to-face, such as checking out groceries in a supermarket, put 100% in that slot.

Maybe it's more complex than that. If you need a secretary to handle the text production for the report, estimate the fraction of time that you must interact face-to-face with your secretary to get the job done. Note that the *fraction of time* is the critical part here. Of the total time you spend (or someone else spends) performing this task, how much has to be face-to-face. If you can do it conveniently over the phone, or by telegram, pony express, smoke signals, or other non-face-to-face medium it doesn't count in the face-to-face race.

Notice that the face-to-face requirement may be dependent on the sophistication of the technology available to you. If you don't even have a telephone, you may need a lot of face-to-face interaction. If you have a switchable, full-motion video teleconferencing system on your desktop, then the need for face-to-face interaction on a daily basis may dwindle into insignificance.

If you're uncertain about how much face-to-face interaction is required, try keeping a short log the next time you have to perform that task. Note how long it took to do that task overall and how much of the time you needed to have face-to-face interaction. If you are analyzing one of your employee's tasks, have him/her keep the log.

Don't get carried away by all of this. We are not searching for ultimate truth here, just a first estimate of what goes on in particular jobs.

Other Location Dependence. Now think of the other two of the three location-dependence elements. There are basically two types of necessary location dependence. Type 1, the first of these, encompasses those situations in which specialized or immovable resources are needed for the job, where there are physical security considerations, or where there is something special about a *specific geographic location* that is important.

Type 2 location dependence comprises the circumstances in which it is important to be in *some* location, but the details of where that location is either are not critical or may change from time to time.

Examples of Type 1 dependence are a central file repository (not computerized), a nuclear particle accelerator facility, a major hospital, an airport, a concert hall or a museum, and a large computer center, the latter only being location-dependent for the operators of the computers. Examples of Type 2 are a branch bank, Social Security, or utilities payment office where people from the neighborhood come to transact business, a conference center, a client's offices, and a shopping center. Even in those installations it is quite likely that not all of the people who are there today *need* to be there all of their working time. As in the case of the face-to-face requirement, think of the percent of time people *must* be in a specific location.

Where the tasks involve operations using transportable records, such as paper forms whose contents are to be entered into computer files, it is possible to have delivery and pickup arrangements to homes or telework centers in order to allow telecommuting. For example, a "distribution pool" could be arranged so that one worker could distribute the day's/week's forms to the telecommuters. Or workers living nearby might carry materials back and forth in a "paper pool." Or the materials could be sent to one of the organization's facilities that is a short distance from the employee's home. In some instances the telecommuter will come on site perhaps once or twice a week, to pick up and/or deliver materials and confer with a supervisor and/or co-workers.

Job Design Possibilities. Don't forget some work flow and job design considerations here. For example, let's say that a set of home telecommuters is doing nothing but primary text entry from dictation, while the regular office workers are reduced to correcting the errors of the telecommuters. That is, both groups are given only portions of the overall task, with little means of interaction. This is almost guaranteed to cause scheduling and morale problems. This doesn't mean that telecommuting is inapplicable, only that it takes thoughtfulness in the final application. Those assignments should be reevaluated so that the work flow is uninterrupted and neither group feels thwarted.

Here's an example of what can go wrong if you don't consider such things, quoted from the *Wall Street Journal:*[3]

> *"TELECOMMUTING: Is it fair to those who still must go in to the office?*
>
> Some 27% of the telecommuters' office colleagues say the innovation has increased their workload, reports the Washington State Energy Office. Among the complaints, having to answer phones and deal with walk-ins for the absent telecommuters. Workers at Apple Computer complained that managers tend to overlook telecommuters when it comes to assigning tasks. *Phone mail, better scheduling and training* have helped alleviate such problems.

Back at the spreadsheet, put 100% opposite a task if it *must* be performed in a particular place, either because it needs face-to-face interaction or either type of other location dependency. In the example for Job B, the only 100% dependency is because of the face-to-face requirement for presenting information (the company doesn't have a videoconferencing system).

Put 0% opposite tasks like "Analyzing figures" and "Composing letters and memos" unless there is only one place where these tasks are relevant. One can analyze figures and compose letters and memos anywhere, in principle. On the other hand, if you need some equipment to do those things—and the equipment is only in the main office or a telework center—then enter the percentage of the time you need to use the equipment. Put 100%'s opposite tasks like "Piloting the Plane to Tulsa,"

---

[3] From the Labor Letter column, Tuesday, May 18, 1993. The article goes on to say: "Hewlett-Packard has a different problem: Its telecommuters get too far ahead of their office colleagues on independent work teams." Why is this considered to be a problem? What should be done about it?

"Reading Top Secret Documents," or "Briefing the Board of Directors" (if you don't have a color videoconferencing system in your organization) although the task of *preparing* the briefing might have a 0%.

The chances are that many, if not all, of the tasks you have just reviewed have *a portion* of their content that is both face-to-face and location independent. These are necessary conditions for home-based telecommuting. Telework center telecommuting requirements are less rigorous; Type 2 location dependence may not hinder establishment of either of these. On the contrary, it may enhance it.

HINT. In working with a variety of different organizations, most of which do not have high- or mid-tech options like video teleconferencing or electronic mail available to them, we have found a fairly common set of responses to the location independence question. Managers tend to respond that their own location independence is in the range[4] from 10% to 80%, and averages 40%. Prospective telecommuters' estimates of their own location independence ranges from 20% to 90%, averaging 60%. Thus, the average manager could be somewhere else two of five days per week, while the average telecommuting prospect could be away from a traditional office three out of five days per week, in their estimations.

Getting to the Bottom Line

It's time for the last two columns in your spreadsheet. Label the first one (Column D) "Location Dependence as % of Job." Label the second (Column E) "Location Independence." The rest is simple arithmetic. To get the number in the "Location Dependence as % of Job" column (Column D), simply multiply the number in the % of the Job Column (Column B) by the number in the next column (Column C) and divide by 100. For

---

[4] The ranges quoted here include 90% of the responses; the lower and upper 5% of managers' and prospective telecommuters' responses go to 0 and 100%, respectively.

example, in Table 2-4, for the "Preparing reports" task has Location Dependence as % of Job as (10 × 10/100) or 1. The Dependence Fraction column shows how much of the time you, or your employees, have to be at a certain place.

"The Independence Fraction," the last column, is simply the number in Column B minus the number in Column D; in the case of "Preparing reports" in Table 2-4, that works out to 10 - 1 or 9, which is simply 100% minus the Dependence Fraction. Add all the numbers in the Independence column and you get the theoretical fraction of your (or someone else's job) that is telecommutable. In the case of our example, the number is 67%: two-thirds of the time.

The Reality Factor

It is important to remember that, even though a worker may have a substantial requirement for face-to-face interaction, it may be possible to clump these interactions such that they all occur in one or two days per week, for example. This is easiest to arrange when the required face-to-face interaction is at weekly staff meetings or other regular events. This is most difficult to arrange when the interaction is irregular and/or depends on coordinating schedules of several other people. In the latter case, the proviso must be repeated: *Must* meetings really be face-to-face or could some telecommunications-mediated technique, such as telephone conferencing or electronic mail, serve as an effective substitute for some of the meetings?

It may not be feasible in some offices for the workers to telecommute if they are needed to respond to in-person public or customer inquiries. On the other hand, it is quite feasible with call forwarding, for example, to have telecommuters handle phone inquiries. Further, it may be possible, with cross-training, to rotate those in-person activities among the staff members so that everyone gets a chance to telecommute and no one feels put upon.

One of the main features of telecommuting (particularly home telecommuting when no one else is at home) is that it allows workers to devote relatively long periods to work tasks without the interruptions or fragmentation common in traditional offices. Where a person's job has a relatively high number of these long-duration tasks, or where such tasks as there are can be grouped into one or two days per week, telecommuting might be particularly appropriate.

This question is most crucial for home-based telecommuters: Can these location-dependent portions of all the tasks be arranged so that they clump into one, two, three, or four days per week, on average?

Be careful with this one! There is a great difference between *can* and *will*. At this point the main question is, is it possible, in principle, to arrange your own (or your employees') schedule(s) so that *all* the required face-to-face meetings occur on two (or fewer) days per week? So that all the other location-dependent activities occur on the same two days? On one day? On three days? Put the number of days per week that you *must* devote to these tasks in the last column after the title REALITY FACTOR. Don't forget that this is an *average* estimate that we need here, where the average may be taken over several months. Some weeks may have more, some fewer such days.

All of the jobs for which the bottom line number of groupable days is less than five are potentially telecommutable from home on a regular basis. Even jobs that have an average number of groupable days per week that is between 4 and 5 are telecommutable from home some of the time and, possibly, from a telework center a significant part of the time. Those jobs for which the answer is 5 (or greater) are not suitable for home-based telecommuting. Those people simply have to be in an office somewhere—again, the office could be in a telework center.

For those jobs where there is a *daily Type 1* location dependence, telecommuting of any sort is not a possibility. We estimate that category encompassed about 60% of the total U.S. work force in 1987, shrinking to less than 50% by 1993. That leaves about half of the work force (about 60 million people) whose jobs are candidates for some form of telecommuting, some or all of the time. We also expect that the fraction of telecommutable jobs will increase over the next few decades, because of technological changes.

Output Quality Issues

In some cases of telecommuting, the nature of the output changes. This may be relatively minor, such as the use of laser printers instead of typewriters (the quality differences are small in many moderately priced printers now on the market). A similar possibility is that remote secretarial services, in which dictation is being transcribed for printing elsewhere, may have difficulties in switching paper forms between individual documents. A solution to this is to adopt common message and letter forms for all of the participating organizational units or, barring that, to include letterhead printing (for example) as a routine accessory in the finished product. Our experience has been that the acceptance of general (or computer-stored-format) forms is rapidly increasing as personal computers become common.

In other cases the product is different, such as sending informal reports via electronic or voice mail instead of via interoffice memos. These may not be in accordance with established tradition and may cause acceptance problems.

An Incomplete List of Telecommutable Jobs

None of the issues in this section is a fundamental barrier to telecommuting. However, they have caused disruption of other organizations' telecommuting in the past because of their alteration of the organization's culture/quality criteria. Hence these issues should be considered in establishing the final selection.

To give you an idea of what sorts of jobs are appropriate for the different forms of telecommuting, Table 2-5 provides a list of possibilities. Because the Federal list of job titles has thousands of entries, this is necessarily just a rough sketch. For example, our list of telecommutable jobs for the city of Los Angeles government includes more than 400 job classifications, covering almost 16,000 positions.

Is There a Telecommuter Personality?

Aside from the characteristics of a person's job, some people will work out better than others as telecommuters. In telecommuting, as in many job situations there seem to be ideal types of people, particularly for home-based telecommuting. This section concentrates on the psychological factors that are important in successful telecommuting, with emphasis on the home-based telecommuter, since that's the hardest.

Table 2-5: SOME TELECOMMUTABLE JOBS

Job Title	A SAMPLING OF TELECOMMUTABLE JOBS			
	Full-time Home-Based	*Part-time Home-Based*	*Full-time Satellite or Local Center*	*Part-time Satellite or Local Center*
Accountant		☺	☺	☺
Actuary	☺ maybe	☺	☺	☺
Advertising Executive	☺ maybe	☺	☺	☺
Applications Programmer	☺	☺	☺	☺
Architect	☺	☺	☺	☺
Auditor		☺	☺	☺
Author	☺	☺	☺	☺
Bookkeeper		☺	☺	☺
CAD/CAM Engineer		☺	☺	☺
Central Files Clerk			☺ maybe	
Civil Engineer	☺	☺	☺	☺
Clerk-Typist	☺ maybe	☺	☺	☺
Clinical Psychologist			☺	
Computer Scientist		☺	☺	☺
Counter Clerk			☺	
Data Entry Clerk	☺	☺	☺	☺
Data Search Specialist	☺	☺	☺	☺
Department General Manager		☺	☺ maybe	☺
Design Engineer		☺	☺	☺
Economist	☺ maybe	☺	☺	☺
Financial Analyst	☺	☺	☺	☺
General Secretary		☺	☺	☺
Graphic Artist	☺	☺	☺	☺
Industrial Engineer		☺	☺	☺
Journalist	☺	☺	☺	☺
Laboratory Director		☺	☺ maybe	
Laboratory Scientist			☺ maybe	☺ maybe
Lawyer	☺ maybe	☺	☺	☺
Mail Clerk			☺	
Mainframe Operator			☺ maybe	
Maintenance Technician		☺	☺	☺
Manager of Managers		☺	☺	☺
Manager of People		☺	☺	☺
Mgr., Machine Systems	☺ maybe	☺	☺	☺
Market Analyst	☺	☺	☺	☺
Marketing Manager		☺	☺	☺
Natural Scientist		☺	☺	☺
Office Machine Operator			☺	
Personnel Manager		☺	☺	☺
Purchasing Manager	☺ maybe	☺	☺	☺
Radio Newscaster	☺	☺	☺	☺
Realtor	☺	☺	☺	☺
Receptionist			☺	
Risk Analyst	☺	☺	☺	☺
School Administrator		☺	☺	☺
Software Engineer	☺	☺	☺	☺
Statistician	☺ maybe	☺	☺	☺
Stock Analyst	☺	☺	☺	☺
Stock Broker	☺	☺	☺	☺
Supervisor	☺ maybe	☺	☺	☺
Systems Engineer		☺	☺	☺
Systems Programmer		☺	☺	☺
Technical Writer	☺	☺	☺	☺
Telemarketer	☺	☺	☺	☺
Telephone Operator	☺	☺	☺	☺
Theoretical Physicist	☺	☺	☺	☺
Traveling Salesperson		☺	☺	☺
University Professor		☺	☺	☺
Word Processing Secretary	☺	☺	☺	☺

Telecommuter Traits

The ideal home-based telecommuter is a person who is strongly self-motivated and self-disciplined, who has all the required skills for his or her job, who has a home environment all set up for telecommuting and who is enthusiastic about the prospects. Since it is possible that not all of your employees fall immediately into this category, here are some of the key characteristics to consider.

Self-Motivation. Since home-based telecommuters do not have the visual and aural cues of the traditional office to keep them motivated—and may have distractions that are not in the traditional office—the more internal drive they have to get the job done, the easier it is to adjust to telecommuting. With some workers this motivation is apparent. With others it may be latent, appearing in strength when they are given the chance. Motivation can still be supplied externally, as discussed in later sections on technology, but the self-starter characteristic is an important one.

Self-Discipline. Of comparable importance is self-discipline. Even if a worker is highly motivated it can all come to nothing if self-discipline is lacking. Since a home-based telecommuting environment is not amenable to constant monitoring[5] it is much better to have workers who do not need it. As in the case above it often happens that people who may need frequent urging in the traditional office can adapt readily to a home telecommuting environment. The key derives from the fact that they can work at their own pace and in their own style, and they have new feelings of responsibility.

THE WEIRD PART IS I DON'T EVEN LIKE CARROTS...

Job Skills and Experience. The smoothest transition to home-based telecommuting is with a person who already has the skills and experience to do the job. In some cases the skills part can be addressed by some additional training, but this should be assessed *before* active telecommuting begins. The need for specific job experience is less certain. We have found that individuals with comparable experience, but who may be new to a particular job—or even to the organization—can function effectively as home-based telecommuters. An efficient electronic mail system might help greatly in this respect, once they have passed the initial familiarization stages.

---

[5] Actually, it *is* technologically possible to monitor home telecommuters continuously. We strongly recommend against it for reasons of good management practice, not to mention invasion of privacy issues.

Flexibility and Innovativeness. Telecommuting is a new way of working. Employees who generally have difficulty adjusting to new situations may also have difficulty in a telecommuting environment. Employees who are innovative and flexible in their attitudes will likely have little or no difficulty adapting.

Socialization. Home-based telecommuting—and to a lesser extent, satellite and local center telecommuting—places restrictions on the amount and scope of face-to-face socializing that can be contained within a job. To some extent this can be replaced, or even surpassed, by electronic forms of communication, but it is clearly a different situation than the traditional office environment. The office is a social arena in addition to its nominal function as a place for business to occur. Frequently the informal communication that occurs during office socializing is as important as formal office communication. On the other hand, some people do much better without the socializing that ordinarily goes on in an office. The key here is to facilitate necessary social exchange while paying less attention to unnecessary interaction. There are also the factors of introversion and extroversion to be considered. People who are very extroverted are not likely to make good frequent home telecommuters. Most people fall in a middle range, desiring some time to be left alone, at other times wanting to be with other people.

The policy of selecting volunteers for telecommuting generally eliminates those people who strongly desire always to be with others and who are very other-directed. Part-time home telecommuting takes care of most of the intermediate situations. Therefore, these criteria should be used primarily to indicate *relative* needs for face-to-face interaction that is in addition to task-related communications. Often, additional social needs can be met by informal group meetings after work.

Life Cycle Stage. In addition to characteristic personality traits, many successful home telecommuters are at stages in their lives when working at home has positive tradeoffs. As a counterexample, young singles who depend on peer contact to meet and form social relationships want to be on site around the coffee machine or in the hallways or cafeteria with access to a pool of potential leisure, as well as work friends.

At other times in their lives these same workers may enjoy being able to work in their homes where they can spend "break" times with their children, a retired spouse or neighborhood friends. This may be a particularly good way to attract valued retirees who still want to spend part-time working.

The Family. Home telecommuters should not be considered in isolation from their families (however you may wish to interpret "family"). The family environment while a telecommuter is working at home becomes the surrogate for the office environment. If work disruptions from the family become intrusive, productivity and morale can fall. If the family environment is supportive, productivity and morale can soar.

The primary issue here is whether the worker can come to a satisfactory working relationship with his or her family at home. The best approach to this at the screening stage is to point out some of the problems of family interaction, such as interruptions for non-work activities, leisure-work conflicts, schedule or space conflicts with family members, and "break-in time" expectations. As a key example, home telecommuting is *not* a satisfactory substitute for child care, particularly with very young children. A home telecommuter with a young child either will require someone available to take care of the child while he or she is working or will have to adjust his or her work schedule around the child's active periods (say, between midnight and 2:00 A.M.?).

Compulsions. Some home telecommuters have found themselves affected by various compulsions that they were able to forestall in their previous office environments. They find themselves giving way to these drives when in an isolated environment such as home. These compulsions include overeating, drug abuse, and workaholism. For most people there are countervailing pressures at home, or they develop new self-disciplines to fight them. However, some telecommuters may succumb. As in the case of family-related issues, the screening process should consist primarily of cautions about the possibilities rather than questions about workers' possibly compulsive habits.

Physical Environment for Home Telecommuting. Although this is not strictly a socio-psychological issue, it is important to require at least some location in the telecommuter's home that is suitable for an office during working hours. It is preferable, but not mandatory, that this be a permanent location, not requiring daily set-up and take-down. If there is no place that can be isolated during working hours (whatever those may be), then the likelihood of successful long-term telecommuting is very small.

These May Be Better Off in the Office

From the list above, a pattern appears for people who would be better off in a formal/traditional office environment. This can often be in a satellite or local center, so it doesn't necessarily preclude people from telecommuting. But clearly people who need direct physical supervision, for reasons of motivation or discipline, should not be assigned home-based telecommuting jobs.

People who are great socializers, who need face-to-face interaction with others to function well, should stick to the office. People who are inflexible in their work habits, the stereotypical bureaucrats, may have difficulty working at home. Young singles who also use the office or its environs as a mate-meeting opportunity similarly may prefer the office to home. Substance abusers, assuming their sources of supply are equally available, may get worse if they are home-based telecommuters. (They may also get better if the office figured as one of the irritants motivating them to their abuse. In any case they should get treatment!) One of the substances most abused by home-based telecommuters was once thought to be food. Our evidence is that few telecommuters experience any significant weight gain or loss.

As you consider these factors, also remember that most home-based telecommuters will only be at home part-time. The rest of the time they will be in an office in which many of the needs just mentioned will be satisfied.

Try Some and See

None of the factors just discussed is an absolute predictor of potential telecommuting performance. It is possible, if unlikely, that apparently ideal telecommuters won't work out. It is also possible, or maybe less unlikely, that people who you might think wouldn't work out as telecommuters will do just fine. We suggest that your implementation strategy go as follows:

- Pick some of your best candidates for telecommuting to start as your seed team. If you have a satellite facility, start there.

- Then, as you develop experience managing them, have some work at home and add some of your less-telecommutable employees. You will pick up your own clues as to what does and does not work for you as you go along.
- Keep adding telecommuters until you feel you have reached a reasonable limit—or until you have run out of employees. We keep being surprised at the variety of people who are successful home-based telecommuters.

The Selection Procedure

A formal selection procedure consists of identifying potential participating organizational units and volunteers within those units. The basis for individual selection is the series of considerations just outlined. Here are some schedule and administrative details.

Volunteers Only!

I suggest that you first identify the potential participating organizational units, then select individual participants, using the screening criteria described below, rather than ask for volunteers in general and then reject some. In any case the criteria described here are intended to enhance the likelihood of success of the project, not to provide a comprehensive survey of all the possible cases where telecommuting may, or may not, work well. You are likely to find that the number of volunteers grows after your first group has been telecommuting for a while. Those of your employees who were initially against it, or were uncertain, may well change their minds as the risks they imagined fail to appear.

Evaluating Jobs and Work Groups

We suggest that you start by identifying the organizational units that have the largest number of potential telecommuters by virtue of the willingness of their managers to participate, the job characteristics of the members of the units, and the economic leverage telecommuting might provide, in that order. If you have only one unit, your own, that part is easy. Go through the job characteristics in some detail. JALA International has developed a computer program, called *Telepicker*, that automates the process on an individual basis.

Details

The following describes in more detail the selection procedure that was outlined earlier.

Jobs

First, the jobs. Here it is important to wrench your mind away from thinking about the details of how each job is done today. Think about the *content* of each of your employees' jobs. What really has to happen to make that job work? What sort of results does the job produce? Can you recognize the results easily—typed memos, reports, lines of software code, engineering drawings? What is it, exactly, that you use to evaluate the employee's work? How often are these discernible products produced? What sorts of skills are required to produce the products? What sorts of resources are needed to get the job done? With whom—or what—must the worker communicate to get or send the information necessary for good performance? How frequently must that communication occur? How "rich" does the communication have to be?

Think of each person as a community, or a factory if you're mechanically minded. Each one requires inputs of materials and information at regular intervals, sometimes continuously, other times sporadically. Each one contains a number of different actors, agents, or do-ers. Each of those is busy some of the time, not so at others. So what we see is great burst of visible activity at times, while at other times everything seems to be dormant—resting, ruminating, developing, re-energizing. No job, unless it's incredibly boring, is the same thing all the time. What we're after is to get a feel for the relative concentrations of activities that can be done alone—or alone with telephone, versus the ones that have to be done someplace, with someone else. If you think the alone-with-phone jobs can be lumped into whole days at a time, you have identified a home-telecommutable job. Make a list of the candidates.

Table 2-6: JOB LOCATION REQUIREMENT EXAMPLES

Full-time At Principal Office	Part-time At Principal Office	Full-time At Some Office	Part-time At Some Office	No Significant Office Requirement
Counter Clerk; Mainframe Operator	Accountant; Most Managers	Field Engineer; Most information workers	Many Professionals; Administrative Assistant	Super-Specialists; Sales Reps

The criteria for satellite center telecommuting are much less exacting. Most jobs can probably be done at a properly equipped satellite center, with the exception of those with distinct physical security or specialized equipment restrictions, *provided* that they also do not require relatively constant face-to-face interaction among specific people.

Make a list like the one in Table 2-6 for the jobs in your group. In Column 1 are the jobs that must be done in the *principal* office *all* of the time. In Column 2 are the jobs that must be done in the *principal* office *some* of the time. In Column 3 are the jobs that must be done in *some* office *all* of the time. In Column 4 are the jobs that must be done in *some* office *some* of the time. *Some* here means at least one day per week. If there are any jobs left in your group list, they could belong to full-time home telecommuters in Column 5. Remember, at this point we're talking about *jobs*, not *people*. If all your jobs are in Column 1, stop. You need go no further; there is no possibility for telecommuting in your group (assuming you listed your own job as well). For the other columns there are increasing possibilities for home telecommuting.

Now, some of those jobs may still require that there be regular face-to-face communication between specific other jobs. That is, there may still be groups of jobs that are geographically inseparable. Move them into Columns 1 or 2 even if they started out in 3, 4, or 5. That should complete your list of dispersible jobs.

People

Next, put the real live people in the jobs. How well do you think they would function away from the principal office? *How often do they need your personal supervision? How often do you need to see them to do your job?*

If your thoughts in this line make you tend to move some more people to Column 1, *stop*. Is that because they need more training, are difficult to communicate with, are unreliable, are unmotivated, or what? Is the problem unapproachable or can it be improved by a new job or changes in the details of the job? If it seems insoluble, move the job/person toward Column 1. Otherwise, this may be a good opportunity to improve that person's situation. Also consider the option that you might have a group of first telecommuters that you can add to as time passes and your and their experiences develop.

After all of this soul-searching you have a list as follows: Column 1 includes those who simply must be in the principal office almost all of the time. Column 2 has the people who must be in the principal office some of the time but could be part-time telecommuters from a satellite office or from home (you might want to have columns 2a and 2b to decide which). Column 3 contains the satellite office telecommuters. Column 4 has those that might share time between satellite office and home, and Column 5, if any, has the potential full-time home telecommuters—or those who might be *really* far away, such as in a distant city. For all of these, the term *all of the time* should be interpreted liberally. For practical purposes, *all of the time* means an average of four days per week (or more), not *forever*.

Discussing the Options

Most of the above cannot be done unilaterally. It is important to discuss the possibilities of telecommuting with all of those people who are likely to be directly involved, whether or not they will all be telecommuters. The first step may be a briefing to all of the potential managers of telecommuters, followed by a similar one to prospective telecommuters themselves. Each of these briefings should contain at least the following topics:

- What telecommuting is as it applies to us
    from home
    from a telework center (if applicable)
- The criteria for telecommuters, for example:
    discuss the screening quiz
- The volunteer nature of telecommuting;
- Advantages and disadvantages of telecommuting, both at home and at satellite centers; myths and realities
- Responsibilities of home telecommuters
- The practical realities
    equipment
    working environment

Don't go overboard at this stage. This is just a briefing to acquaint people with telecommuting in a realistic way. The training briefings for the actual telecommuters come later. *It is important at this stage to stress that telecommuting is neither a privilege nor a penalty for those involved—just a different way of working.*

Final Selection

Now for the decision-making. We suggest that you give a formal screening test[6] to all the volunteers that you—and their supervisors—have identified. The test will provide an evaluation of the likely success of each individual as either a home or satellite telecommuter. The formal evaluation is not the final word. It is an input for your own decision. Is this person a good candidate for telecommuting? There will be some clear yeses, possibly some equally clear negatives, and likely some borderline cases. Generally, fewer than 15% of the potential telecommuters get a "no telecommuting" recommendation from such tests, but those may be important *nos*.

We suggest that you keep in mind our earlier advice: Try some of the borderline people as well as the definite winners. Sometimes the feeling of added responsibility will convert them into your star performers.

---

[6] You may want to invent your own, based on the material discussed here. Otherwise, JALA International, Inc. has a standard screening test service that has been used for thousands of telecommuters.

3

Site Location

There are basically two types of fixed locations from which one can telecommute: one's home or an office somewhere. This chapter discusses the general management issues of deciding the mix of locations that is appropriate for your organization.

In 1989, we surveyed about one thousand information workers who were employed by a large California organization. One of the survey's purposes was to develop a feel for the likely distribution of telecommuting sites for that employer. That is, about how many could work at home, how many from a telework center, and how many would be required to keep commuting to their principal office. The survey questions were taken from a questionnaire we use routinely to assess the likely telecommutability of individuals. The questions considered only the job content, not the behavioral issues of telecommuting. None of the individuals questioned had received any prior information about telecommuting.

We found that about 20% of the respondents to that general survey would be able to telecommute at least part-time from home; 50% would be able to telecommute from a telework center; and the remaining 30% might have to remain at the principal office. A careful review of the answers of that last 30% leads me to believe that about half of them could work effectively at a telework center.

That conclusion also matches the results from our usual

screening surveys of pre-briefed telecommuting candidates: About 15% would still have to work full-time at the principal office, while 30% could telecommute from home some of the time. Note that none of these surveys assumed a technology level greater than that of the late 1980s in a middle- to low-tech organization.

So, the chances are that, in your company, somewhere between 70% and 85% of the information workers could be telecommuters, based on their reported location independence. The practical split between home and telework center depends on the details of managment practices and the physical characteristics of the respective sites.

Homes

In most work situations, the condition, size, and location of an employee's home are unrelated to whatever goes on at work; as a manager you probably never even think about it. Further, there is a general feeling that employers should not interfere with employees' home lives.

Who Decides?

But whether a prospective telecommuter's home is suitable for telecommuting has to be a critical decision in the site selection process. Is it an equally or more suitable environment (as compared to the principal office) for perfoming useful work? Or is it likely to be a place with distractions that are more powerful than at the principal office? How can you know?

The obvious way to find out is to inspect the premises. The obvious policy question is whether you, as an employer, even want to inspect the homes of all of your current or prospective home-based telecommuters. Some employers insist on it, as part of their plan for minimizing liability risk. Most simply reserve the right to inspect a telecommuter's home, after giving appropriate notice, and require that each telecommuter agrees to keep his or her home in a condition no more hazardous than that in the principal office. That is, you explain the requirements to the telecommuters and trust them to adhere to them.

As an aid to making that decision, here is a general overview of home office standards. Chapter 9 has more on the details of home office design.

Home telecommuting is both the easiest and the hardest form of telecommuting in terms of selecting the site. It's the easiest because the location is automatically chosen when the home-based telecommuter is selected; there are no problems of finding the right address. It's the hardest form of telecommuting because homes are definitely not offices. It may take some straining and shoving to get them to be suitable work places. In some parts of the world—such as in most countries other than the United States[1]—no amount of shoving and straining will work; homes are simply too small to contain a permanent office environment in addition to the rest of the household furnishings and necessary living space.

If an employee has sufficient determination, it is possible for that person to telecommute from almost any home situation where there is a reasonable amount of space, even if it is only temporary. But it is more desirable to modify the household space layout in order to provide an "office" space with control over noise, interruptions, work equipment, and materials. What follows are some general parameters for setting up a wide variety of home offices, including criteria for screening[2] domestic environments to anticipate their suitability for business. As a telemanager, you should be aware of these issues, especially the ones that might have legal implications.

Standards for the Physical Setting

Homes are definitely not designed to be offices, although many homes have space designated as office-like—the library or den. The management problem is to increase the likelihood that home-based telecommuters will maximize these attributes, either in the home proper or in outlying buildings:

- adequate work space; at least as much as in the principal office
- access to telephone or electrical outlets, if needed
- security and safety of work materials
- sound control

---

[1] In the US, our average home-based telecommuter lives in a home with about 180 square meters. In Japan and Europe, homes typically have less than 100 square meters of floor space. The typical office space for a mid-level information worker is about 15 square meters.

[2] If "screening" sounds too intrusive, then consider this material as information to be communicated to your telecommuters.

- separation from on-going domestic activities
- temperature and light control

Almost any place in the home is being successfully used for telecommuting now: the basement, attic, the dining room table, a spare bedroom, an outbuilding, and even the kitchen of a mother-in-law who lives next door. What makes the use successful, however, is that during the period of work, the space meets the criteria above.

People who would have chronically conflicting uses of residential space should probably not be accepted as home telecommuters. Even part-time telecommuters should have a permanent space for their work if they share their space with other people. Otherwise they may have significant problems in integrating work with the other household activities—with a resulting loss in productivity and an increase in stress.

However, this caution does not preclude the use of convertible facilities, where the work area may be used for other household purposes during non-working hours. For example, the telecommuter may have a piece of furniture that encloses the computer, monitor, and printer, opening up for work and folding away into a compact, out-of-the-way module at other times.

Many professionals whose work is task-oriented can work at home for the duration of a given project. For those workers it may be enough to continue such present informal practices as taking a notebook computer home, preparing the work on the dining table, and transmitting data from the kitchen where the household telephone is located. *Intermittent home telecommuters should not be disqualified from telecommuting, particularly at the demonstration project stage, since they form a precedent-setting group important in the implementation of formalized telecommuting.*[3]

However, in departments where the periods to be spent telecommuting can be anticipated and found to justify the expense of employer-provided telephone lines and other office equipment, encourage the telecommuter to upgrade the home

---

[3] Most companies still require an average of one telecommuting day per week as a condition of participation in their initial demonstration project. However, someone who telecommutes from home four or five straight days in a month still qualifies under this rule even though s/he is an intermittent telecommuter in this sense.

work space to facilitate uninterrupted work.[4] In many cases, in our experience, the telecommuters are willing to bear the expense of many or all of these additions. Nevertheless, company policy should be explicit on who bears the costs. It also may be useful to publish a list of home office requirements for prospective telecommuters—or have them read Chapter 9.

Who Pays?

In general employers of telecommuters do not provide employer-owned furniture or equipment for home office installation for telecommuting, although some may provide allowances or purchase discounts for telecommuting employees. The office at home, as at work, should be equipped with furniture and lighting appropriate to the tasks performed. You can't expect high levels of productivity from a worker stressed by aching arms and back, strained eyes and ears, or other discomforts. Special attention must be given to employees working in home offices at computer monitors because poor positioning of the keyboard and screen relative to the worker's body can cause extreme fatigue.

Telework Centers

Telework centers resemble conventional office environments. However, there are some key differences. Final selection among the many possible combinations of sites depends heavily on the geography of the implementation city, the location of participant residences, the need for face-to-face meeting sites, and, of course, budget constraints.

Selection Issues

We usually screen potential telecommuters in order to divide them into two groups: home (mostly) and telework center telecommuters. Telework center telecommuter candidates are those who:

- indicate a preference for telework center telecommuting, or

---

[4] This move also brings up a legal question: Who owns the changes and/or additional equipment? What happens if the telecommuter quits the company—or just quits telecommuting? Most companies simply write off the installation expense, provided that it is fairly modest. Nevertheless, this is a point that should be considered by the legal staff *before* telecommuting begins.

whose equipment/facilities requirements or job/behavioral characteristics do not favor home-based telecommuting; and

- work in organizations willing to operate with (or test the utility of) telework center employees; and
- live within a *reasonably* short distance of a potential center.

The term "reasonably" above will vary. At one extreme, any center that reduces employee commute times by one-quarter or more might do. At the other end, the goal may be to have all telework center telecommuters walk or bicycle to work. In the first case, the center may still be ten miles or more from the average telecommuter's residence. In the other case, it may be around the corner, on a different floor of the high-rise apartment building, or within a few blocks of home. In the 1990s, I expect to see all of these evolve, slowly moving toward a global network of home offices and telework centers, covering an entire spectrum of sizes.

The next step is to arrive at a list of potential sites, in the cases where telework centers appear to be desirable. Ideally, telework centers would be located in or near clusters of current and/or prospective employee residences. In practice, current company ownership or lease agreements for candidate facilities close to the ideal locations would be used to select the prospective sites, where possible. Long-term leases with large unexpired portions certainly can limit the flexibility of site location unless subletting space is a real possibility.

It might also be useful to explore and evaluate one or more of the several forms of decentralized site mentioned in Chapter 1, including the following, ranging from the largest to the smallest in size:

1. A conventional telework complex totally occupied by company workers and otherwise indistinguishable from a central location office building, except that workers would report to the office on the basis of their residence locations rather than their organization headquarters locations
2. As above, except that the buildings might be shared by other firms in additional to company units
3. Neighborhood office centers, such as "store-front" units, in which only a few workers would work and which would be located in the immediate neighborhoods of the workers' residences.

Final site selection may also involve some design issues. For example, the project might have a situation in which telecommuters are at home much of the time but also require some private, possibly shared office space plus conference facilities for periodic meetings. There are also some internal space design issues related to the extent of computer use at the centers. For example, centers where there is intensive computer use and large amounts of data sharing may require provisions for extra communications network cabling. This requires a different sort of office design than is traditional in buildings housing pre-computer-age information workers.

Telework Centers versus Conventional Office Environments

While relocating an entire organizational unit from a central office to a telework center may be useful in evaluating some aspects of decentralization (e.g., relative lease costs of central versus suburban sites), unless everyone in this organizational unit lives a short distance from the center location, the exercise does little to explore some of the more important dimensions of the problem (e.g., effect of telecommuting on transportation patterns). In fact, the move of an entire organizational unit to another location almost always causes more disruption, loss of key personnel, morale crashes and other costs than it is worth in facilities rental savings.[5]

Individuals, Not Organizations

Therefore, most telework centers will accommodate a group of employees whose only other connection is that they live in close proximity to the center. This differs from a common misconception of a telework office, which considers a telework facility as reserved for whole departments or otherwise entire work units.

Shared Support Personnel and Services

Unlike the traditional setting where clerical and other support functions are contained in the organizational unit, the telework center may have personnel performing these services for the diversity of occupants of the center. Or the services may be performed entirely from other sites via telephone and electronic mail connections. Similarly, I anticipate that support spaces and equipment such as conference areas and photocopy machines will be utilized on a shared basis. One set of privately operated telework centers in California has an extensive automatic system for machine-use and support service personnel accounting for its tenants (about 70% of whom were telecommuters in 1992.)

In fact, one possibility is to have a telework center that consists solely of meeting and support equipment facilities, with minimal or no permanent support staff at the center. In this arrangement, the telecommuters would work from home much of the time, coming to the telework center only for meetings or for use of the support equipment.

In particular, I suggest that the company provide the basic support services/equipment and the site manager for each telework center. The role of site manager is described more fully in Chapter 6. The site manager's job is that of overseeing the process of activities at the site: availability of supplies and support services, attendance of teleworkers, maintenance of security, and so on. The site manager is *not* responsible for evaluation of the performance of employees from other

---

[5] For a more detailed explanation of this, see *Telecommunications and Organizational Decentralization* by Jack M. Nilles, IEEE Transactions on Communications, Vol. COM-23, No. 10, October 1975, pp. 1142–1147.

organizations, except in an advisory capacity to the functional managers of the telecommuters at the site.

Size

At present, most operating telework centers have fewer than 100 occupants, although the center may be shared with other units of the company which are located in the traditional mode. For example, a storefront office in an older neighborhood could be as suitable for a center as a new suburban office building. A telework center might also occupy leased space in a conventional office building amid other tenants. Some Pacific Bell telework centers are located in buildings that formerly were filled with telephone switching equipment; digital switches occupy much less space, thereby allowing the rest of the building to be used for other purposes. The major requirements are suitable space to accommodate people and work activities, and ease of space alteration to satisfy architectural requirements.

Distribution of Telecommuters Between Home Offices and Telework Centers

The distribution of telecommuters depends on the outcome of the screening process. As a first approximation, if you're just starting a telecommuting program, you might want half of the company's telecommuters working from home, the other half from one or more telework centers.

Clearly, another major option is available. Many telecommuters who nominally work at home could also be part-time telework center workers. They could spend most of their time either at home or at a telework center, with only occasional excursions to their unit's central office (if it is not at the telework center). Hence we might have all of the telecommuters as telework center workers at least some of the time. The exact final distribution depends on the results of the combined personnel, organization, site selection process.

Selection Criteria for Telework Centers

The need for locating telework centers close to residences to minimize travel time is readily apparent. If you're trying to get employees out of their cars for commuting, I recommend a somewhat arbitrary limit of one mile as the maximum distance from a telecommuter's home to the telework center in which he or she works. In some cases,[6] such as where a number of employees live at great distances from the main office, it might be desirable to relax the maximum limit and put a "half-way office" into operation.

Transportation-Locational Decisions

The easiest way to get this information is to develop a map of employee residence locations by postal Zip code. That is, for each Zip code area in the city, find out how many employees live there. Use your personnel files to get the Zip data. Pick the one or two Zip areas that have the highest density of employee/telecommuter residences and find a suitable office site in or near the center of those areas. An "eyeball" choice is usually adequate to locate a prospective area.[7]

If you want to establish or participate in neighborhood telecenters, then Zip codes probably provide too coarse a filter. You may have to resort to mapping the actual residence locations of your employees to find the best spots that are within walking distance of their homes.

In accordance with Murphy's (or Parkinson's) law, if you have multiple facilities now, then it seems that employees who live in the East side commute to the West side while the people who live in the West side commute to the East. If this is the case in your company you might wish to locate new centers or rearrange your existing facilities to minimize that travel. It's also worth considering changing job assignments so that the West siders have jobs associated with the West side, and so on.

Parking

Availability of adequate parking (for cars or bicycles, depending on the location) may be an important criterion for the selection of sites and facilities for telework centers.

We do not expect the home office part of telecommuting to create major additional demands for parking in residential areas.

---

[6] Probably most cases in a new telecommuting program in a mid- to large-sized city.

[7] This may be easier said than done. In our work with the City of Los Angeles, out of more than 800 prospective telecommuters in a demonstration project, we found that the highest density Zip area contained residences of only 8 of those employees.

It is conceivable, however, that 50 to 100 new workers at a regional telework center, if they still drive to work, could overtax the available parking in certain settings (e.g., an older commercial strip), with major impacts on the surrounding neighborhood. Therefore, the availability of adequate parking should be one determinant of site selection (although what is "adequate" is still open to definition).

From another point of view, elimination of parking space, since close-in telecommuters may elect not to drive to work, may be an important benefit. It could be worth encouraging employees either to walk, bicycle, take the bus, car or van pool or otherwise not drive to work alone.

Laying Out the Center Space

Space For Work Activities And Support Services

I expect a typical office space requirement for the telework center of approximately 160 square feet per person. This figure includes support space such as corridors and storage areas. So, a telework center for 100 employees would require about 16,000 gross square feet of space. Net square feet, referring to usable office space, would be less, in the order of 145 to 150 square feet per worker.

This estimate is for planning and initial costing purposes only. The final number will depend on such factors as the amount of office sharing done by part-time teleworkers, the ratio of conference room to office space and the amount of shared facilities needed (reception areas, printers, photocopiers, etc.).

Space Arrangements

If the center primarily is to house full-time telecommuters then it will probably be laid out like a traditional office building. The main difference might be in some additional conference space. If, as is more often the case, it is to accommodate a mix of full-time, part-time, and "drop-in" telecommuters, the space requirements are somewhat different.

For example, regular part-time telecommuters might share office space with those who telecommute on other days of the week. A Monday-Wednesday-Friday telecommuter might share space with a Tuesday-Thursday person without running into other than occasional occupancy conflicts. Often, the part-time center telecommuters will be there mostly for meetings, so that their major need is for conference space, together with access to a small office (possibly with-computer) for telephoning or other electronic messaging. So this kind of center would likely have more conference space and less office space than the traditional office building.

Similarly, you may wish to provide office/conference space for drop-in telecommuters: those from other areas or cities who may be in town on business, or for telecommuters who work primarily somewhere else but who come to the center occasionally.

The initial layout of the center, then, depends on an analysis of the numbers of telecommuters who fit into these categories: full-time, part-time shared space, part-time mostly for meetings, and drop-in. It is difficult to forecast all of this up front so the plan should allow for some alteration of space as experience with telecommuting develops. You might want to follow the old maxim for laying out sidewalks—watch where the natural trails develop, then pave them—but apply this to office/conference/support space demands.

Ease of Alteration of Leased Sites

One major cost factor in the leasing of office space is the cost of altering facilities to meet functional and other requirements. For this reason, and because you may have a higher than usual demand for altering the initial layout, the inexpensive adaptation of candidate facilities for telework centers is another important criterion for site selection. It is not anticipated that, with the exception of telecommunications installation, renovation costs for a telework center will be different from the typical renovation costs for traditional leased space.

Telecommuting and Technology

One main theme of this book is that a substantial amount of telecommuting can be accomplished effectively with only a telephone, paper and pencil as the relevant technologies. Yet, application of more sophisticated technology generally makes life easier, increases the amount of telecommuting one can do, and makes telecommuting available to more people. This chapter is about the impacts of technology on telecommuting.

General Rules of Technology

We don't discuss the technology here at the level of detail of brand names, model numbers, or prices. The reason is simple. Information technology (computers and telecommunications) improves, in terms of performance per dollar spent—or decreases in cost per unit of capability, at an *annual* rate of between 25% and 30%. That is, the universal cosmic gadget that you paid $400 for this year will probably sell for about $300 next year, if it isn't already obsolete. So, the process of turning a manuscript into a book that is manufactured and widely distributed, fast though it is, is too slow to keep up with technology details. Any market details printed here would be out of date by the time you read them.

Having said that, I assure you that the *trends* in information technology development are well established. Therefore, it is fairly easy to forecast what *level* of technology you can expect to have available in the year X—and its approximate price, where X is in the next ten or twenty years or so. Of course, there are technological surprises that can alter this forecast, but history has tended to show more positive surprises than disappointments. This leads us to **Technology Rule One**:

> If a certain form of information technology is available today, but costs twice as much as you think you can afford to pay, wait a couple of years; it will be down to your price threshold. If it currently costs ten times as much as you think you can afford, wait about seven years.

This is simply a restatement of the trend mentioned in earlier paragraphs. In Rule One we're talking about *hardware* technology; things like maxi-, mainframe, mini-, and micro-computers; telecommunications media, such as fiber optics lines and satellite dishes; and all the gadgets that plug into them. *Software* tends to follow more obscure rules. Suffice it to say that the great new software package that will finally help you to do that tricky part of your job will take from two to five times as long to appear as the manufacturers initially claim. Hence the well-deserved term *vaporware*.

Nevertheless, the software will finally show up, and of a quality sufficient to make it worth your investment. This leads to **Technology Rule Two**:

> *Always buy the best technology available to accomplish a certain job, even if it stretches your budget slightly.* It is at least a partial guarantee that the technology will still be usable in three years. Don't count on more than a three- to five-year useful lifetime for computers or telecommunications interface equipment (such as modems), for other than very routine[1] information tasks.

However, all of the foregoing doesn't really have much impact on the fundamental telecommutability of large numbers of jobs. It does have a major impact on some jobs, specifically those that need the latest high-powered hardware and software to

---

[1] Keep in mind that what is *routine* is also a moving target. Not so many years ago, secretaries did not routinely compile or update spreadsheets or perform sophisticated document processing. Now, with the aid of inexpensive technology, they do.

keep ahead of the game. This leads to **Technology Rule Three**:

> *The absence of a particular technology, beyond the fundamentals, is rarely a reason (or excuse) not to telecommute.* Almost everyone can telecommute at least part of the time without any form of "advanced" technology. However, improvements over the fundamentals may enable both significant qualitative and quantitative improvements in telecommuting.

All of the rules above have to do with deciding the level of technology required in a closed system. By that we mean, all other things being equal, you only have to worry about Rules One through Three. But, in many situations it is not the case that all other things are equal; you exist in a competitive environment. If you are in that situation, you also have to consider **Technology Rule Four**:

> *Given equal human and economic resources, the person who has the technology best suited for the job wins.* If you are able to do the work faster, with higher quality, at lower cost, or with less strain than your competitor, then you have a competitive advantage. The key question is: Is the cost of the additional technology less than the value of the increased competitive advantage? If it is, then the expenditure could be warranted.

At the same time, don't forget that new technology can have a price significantly beyond its purchase cost: *time*. First, it takes time to learn how to use it to do the tasks for which you purchased it. Often, the technology fails to meet your expectations in one or more respects. As a result, less time than expected is shaved from those established tasks that the technology was supposed to help. In extreme cases, that user surliness may make you take even longer to do the task with the "improved" technology than without it.

Second, it takes even more time to invent new things to do with the technology, or to learn how to do them. Third, the cost of producing the "improved" results may exceed the benefits received. How many times have you spent extra minutes or hours at the computer unnecessarily tweaking that letter or spreadsheet, with no discernible difference to the famous bottom line?

But telecommuting does have an effect on that process, as stated in **Technology Rule Five**:

Telecommuting generally decreases the start-up costs of adoption of a new technology, computer-based technologies in particular.

This is partially the result of greater accessibility. Many offices still have fewer than one personal computer per computer user. In those cases, at least for home-based telecommuters who have personal computers at home, learning the new technology—and inventing new applications for it—is done mostly at home rather than in the principal office.

I have been told repeatedly by telecommuters that the ability to try a new technology at home, without the fear of embarrassment by the snickering power users at the principal office, can be a powerful incentive to someone who is technology-wary. Hence, the learning and innovation time is significantly compressed. This is one of the components of the improved effectiveness demonstrated by telecommuters. Further, the increased emphasis on specifying results (rather than concentrating on a specific procedure that may or may not produce the results) tends to diminish the amount of time wasted in output overkill. Rule Five is particularly important in organizations that ordinarily under-train their employees; that is, most U.S. organizations.

Technology Rule Six is critical:

The technology needed for full-scale successful telecommuting is roughly the same as that required in the principal office—plus some more telecommunications.

No magic here. If you *regularly* need it in the office, you will probably need it in the home office or telework center. The hidden benefit here is that there may be no need for *duplicate* technology. A combination of "older" technologies, such as voice mail and paging, combined with computer sharing in the principal office, possibly with removable hard disks, portable computers for telecommuters and/or telecommuter ownership of their own machines, can make the actual startup cost of technology for telecommuting range from quite low to nonexistent.

You should also keep in mind **Technology Rule Seven:**

Telecommunications networks are the freeways of telecommuting.

If your organization is not extensively intra-connected by digital telecommunications networks now, it soon will be. The emergence of increasingly sophisticated telecommunications networks—and increasingly uniform international telecommunications regulatory policies—will make telecommuting and teleworking practical for almost all information workers around the globe in the next decade.

Figure 4-1 *Technology Ownership Rates*

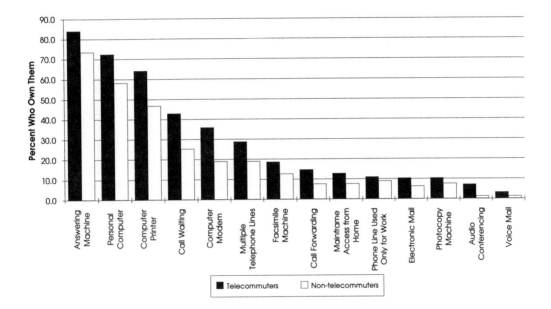

Telecommunications networks for telecommuting can range from the familiar ubiquitous switched telephone system and all its generally available services (call-forwarding, conference calling, call-waiting, voice mail, paging, caller-identification); through the all-digital ISDN (Integrated Services Digital Network) system or switched digital services interconnecting both individuals and arrays of LANs (Local Area Networks); to the next step ATM (Asynchronous Transfer Mode). The mode of telecommunications can be as simple as voice only, or escalate through voice-and-graphics, and various forms of synchronous and asynchronous teleconferencing. Each of these technologies generally follows Technology Rule One, so that a technology that seems to be out of reach today could be business-as-usual in a decade or less.

Finally, lest you get overly excited by all the possibilities out there, observe **Technology Rule Eight**:

> There is no substitute for uniform company technology standards.

At a minimum, the software used by telecommuters should be file-compatible[2] with the software in the principal office. For example, if the principal office uses Macintoshes and one or more telecommuters use PC-compatibles, or vice versa, make sure that one end or the other has software that allows transparent file transfer, either by floppy disk or modem. This problem will recede as more software becomes platform-independent, but it is a common issue in many organizations today.

Keep these rules in mind—or on your wish list—as you decide what technology is required for a given level of telecommuting.

Reality Tests

Brief descriptions or statements of the type of technology needed for telecommuting are scattered throughout this book. The rules just given cover types of technology needed to perform various telecommuting tasks. Now, let's see what is happening at present in non-high-tech, real world organizations.

First, look at some of the results of a survey of a few hundred telecommuters and non-telecommuters, mostly mid-level managers or professionals, concerning the utility of certain types of technology to their work. One test of the importance of a technology is the extent to which it is personally owned/paid for by the telecommuters. Figure 4-1 shows the status late in 1992 for a group of home-based telecommuters and non-telecommuters in a large U.S. metropolitan area, all working for the same large organization. On average, these telecommuters had been working from home for about one year at the rate of slightly more than one day per week.

---

[2] That is, a formatted text, spreadsheet, graphics, or database file produced by machine A should be readable by machine B, whether or not the two machines use the same type of microprocessor to run their programs.

The results in Figure 4-1 must be viewed with some reservations because not all of the technologies, such as voice mail and electronic mail, were readily available to the participants in the survey. Voice mail in particular tends to enhance telecommuting in organizations that have it generally available—yet it is not usually owned by the telecommuters. Further, the survey respondents' jobs covered a very wide spectrum. Some job types are much more dependent than others on a specific technology. Note that price does not seem to be a dominant factor here. Although the most-often-owned technology is answering machines (underlining the importance of voice messaging); personal computers and printers, costing several times as much, rank second. This also demonstrates Rule Six: 74% of these telecommuters owned their own personal computers at the time the survey was made. At the beginning of telecommuting for this organization, half of the applicants already owned their own personal computers.

We also asked the same people how much easier each of these technology types would make their work. The results of that question are shown in Figure 4-2. The scale ran from 1 (it has no effect on my job) to 5 (it makes my job significantly easier).

Figure 4-2 *The Ability of Technology to Make Work Easier*

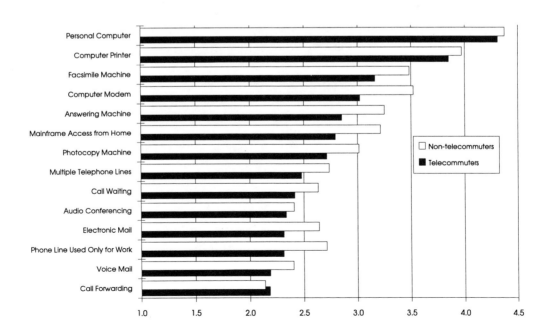

The clear conclusion from these figures is that personal computers, their main peripherals (printers and modems), and facsimile machines should be key components of the future telecommuter's equipage. The differences shown in Figure 4-2 between telecommuters and non-telecommuters are statistically significant only for modems.

Finally, these same telecommuters and non-telecommuters were asked their opinions as to the impact of each of these technology types on increasing the amount of telecommuting they might do from home. The results are shown in Figure 4-3. The asterisks after the names of the technologies indicate that the differences between telecommuters and non-telecommuters are statistically significant.[3]

Figure 4-3 *The Expected Impact of Technology on Increasing Telecommuting*

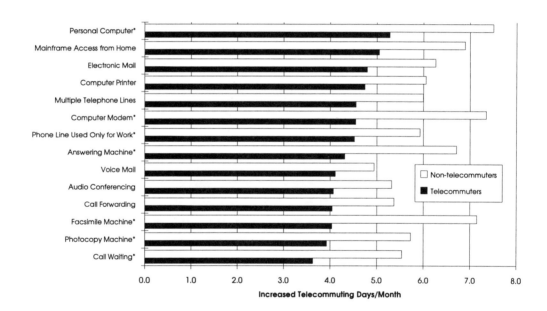

The interesting conclusion to be drawn from the graph is that non-telecommuters have expectations of the effect of technology that are not met in reality. Although both groups feel that added technology would increase the amount of telecommuting that is possible for them, experienced telecommuters are more conservative about the likely extent. This is an empirical test of

_____

[3] At or better than the 0.05 level. This means that the probability that the differences are *not* real is less than 5% for those items with asterisks.

Rule Three above: Lack of a particularly nifty technology may not be as impairing as you might think.

Technology Trends

The previous material concerns the situation in an average-tech organization in the early 1990s. There are some very high-tech organizations using telecommuting, as well as some almost no-tech outfits. All of these are successful in the telecommuting they do. But, as stated earlier, there seems to be a connection between the level and scope of telecommuting in an organization, and the level of technology they use. Here are some general statements about trends in technologies that are particularly suited to telecommuting and to that broader application, teleworking.

Computers

Although about one-third of telecommuters in the late eighties could telecommute at least one day per week without computer assistance, that number has been steadily eroding. Telecommuters are increasingly likely to use computers while telecommuting simply because the percentage of information workers who use computers daily in traditional offices is growing.

Technology Rule One is the main motivator for this. Personal computers are delivering unprecedented information processing power to the desktop, regardless of the location of the desktop. By the year 2000, personal computers will be able to perform almost any task that was mainframe-based in 1990. All of this stems from the growth in power of microprocessors, the "brains" of personal computers. Figure 4-4 tells the story. Similar trends hold for any microelectronics devices, such as memory chips.

In effect, this means that, for most kinds of jobs, the job-holder can soon (if it hasn't happened already) have all the information resources of the principal office at home or in a telework center. Where the telecommunications network can't support enough information transfer, work can be carried between the principal office (if it still exists) and the telework office via some magnetic or optical storage medium. The number of options for this information transfer is continually growing:

floppy disk, removable hard disk, floptical disk, erasable CD-ROM, WORM disk, and PCMCIA[4] storage card, to name a few.

Another critical outcome of this microelectronics capability growth is desktop video conferencing. That is, the average desktop or laptop personal computer of the late 1990s will be able to display the boss and/or the rest of the gang at the principal office in living color, full motion, and stereo sound, given the proper network connections. In early 1994, the cost of point-to-point desktop videoconferencing was about $5,000 per seat. By or before the year 2000, look for a price of about $500 per seat.

Is this an improvement or what? Now the boss can resort to the classical fall-back management technique: Call all the telecommuters and *see* that they look busy. More to the point, lack of visual contact will no longer be an excuse for prohibiting telecommuting.

GOOD MORNING, BOB! NICE TO SEE YOU'RE AT YOUR DESK!

YESSIR!

Further, with multipoint videoconferencing[5] many meetings can be held with all of the participants "present" and no two of them occupying the same room. Will the outcomes be the same as in traditional, everyone-in-the-same-room meetings? We don't know the full answer to that yet, but some outcomes will be better, if only because some meetings would otherwise not be possible, given the schedule conflicts of any group of busy people larger than two.

The danger of all this information processing power is that we can make major mistakes with lightning speed. However, that danger is common to all users of personal computers, not just telecommuters. Many telecommuters have told us that they are far less likely to make computer mistakes while telecommuting because of the major decrease in interruptions, as compared to life in the traditional office.

---

[4] CD-ROM means Compact Disk Read Only Memory; WORM is Write Once Read Only Memory; and PCMCIA is an acronym for Personal Computer Memory Card International Association.

[5] Audio/telephone conferencing can also assist in expanding access to many meetings. Add facsimile and/or computer graphics via modem, and most of the components are there for telemeetings that deal largely with routine information exchange. When the topics get fuzzier, or there is high uncertainty, the need for face-to-face meetings, or a videoconferencing equivalent, increases. However, multipoint videoconferencing is two to three times as expensive as the point-to-point version.

Figure 4-4 *Performance Improvements of Microprocessors*

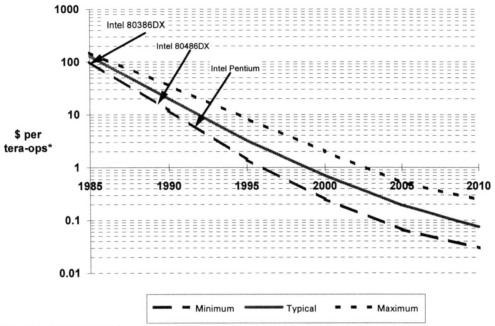

*Trillion gate operations per second

Telecommunications Networks

Telecommunications networks are the freeways of telecommuting. At present there are two broad kinds of networks: local area networks (LANs) and wide area networks (WANs). As the names imply, one concentrates on shipping information around a relatively restricted area, while the other has a much broader scope. You have been using WANs for a long time; the most common WAN is called the telephone system. The problem is that these two kinds of networks encompass a bewildering array of different, and often incompatible technologies, from good old analog voice transmission at 3 kHz to digital data transmission at gigabit-per-second[6] rates.

As far as telecommuting is concerned, the fundamental question is, what has to be telecommunicated? The answer, for most mid-1990 telecommuters, is voice messages, text data and numbers that have been generated "off line." In both of the latter

---

[6] One gigabit per second is a billion 1s and 0s per second.

cases, the text and data are represented on the computer by a small number of bits per information element. Therefore, none of these modes of information transfer requires much in the way of transmission capacity. However, that relatively simple demand on the transmission medium is changing.

One of the key forces for increasing performance demands on telecommunications networks results from the trends in computers: the move toward high-resolution graphical user interfaces (GUIs—pronounced "gooeys"). A GUI can require thousands of times more data than a system that just transmits codes for characters that are displayed on the screen via a character-memory chip. That is, where a DOS character-mode system simply transmits a byte for each character that is displayed on the screen, a GUI system must transmit a picture of that character. This is much more complicated. In addition, GUI systems generally employ color (which further triples the data load) and increasingly complex graphics, so that a super VGA screen requires about 2.4 million bits of data ($1024 \times 768 \times 3$) to display one screenful of information. It needs to do this about 70 times per second. This can be a problem. Even with a modem transmitting at 9600 bits per second, a GUI interface with a distant LAN can seem painfully slow.

Wide Area Networks

The first thing to remember is that good old analog transmission is going away; the telephone system is going digital worldwide, although the transition process may extend into the twenty-first century. The most common telecommuting telecommunications appliance today is the modem. Its sole purpose is to convert the digital output of a computer to analog signals capable of being transmitted on the telephone WAN and vice versa. Various tricks can be used in this process so that a phone line limited to voice transmission (nominally covering the frequency range from 300 Hz to 3 kHz) can be stuffed with 14.4 kilobits per second or more—but not much more. Connecting a high-end personal computer to a modem is sort of like connecting a fire hydrant to a garden hose—lots of ambition but not much production.

The replacement to the Plain Old Telephone System (POTS, for you acronym fanatics) is, first, ISDN (Integrated Services Digital Network) then frame relay and, maybe, ATM (Asynchronous Transfer Mode). All of these WAN technologies are totally digital and deal with message switching. One consequence of this is that you get to throw away your modems and replace them with other interface devices that plug into the phone lines. The more important consequence is that you can send any kind of information over the same telecommunications line—voice, computer data, video—and have it received reliably at the other end, assuming, of course, that the other end knows what to do with it. ISDN networks are in place in many countries around the world and, by the year 2000 should cover most developed countries. Frame relay is a public data network service that can run at speeds up to 1.5 megabits per second. ATM promises to be the next major step past ISDN, with expanded capabilities, but is probably a decade or more away from widespread implementation.

Aside from the message-handling software that constitutes the bulk of ISDN, frame relay, and ATM technology, there is a parallel trend toward replacing copper wires with optical fibers. The motivation is the same as that behind ISDN and ATM developments: increasing capacity—attaching the fire hydrant to a fire hose (the optical fibers) and putting a wetting agent in the water (ISDN and ATM). As of this writing, an interesting contest is developing over who will deliver this capacity to the end users, the established telephone system or cable companies. Whatever the outcome, look for a rapidly growing ability to send any kind of information anywhere at a reasonable price.[7]

The telephone networks aren't the only forms of WAN. There are many other types, from private networks under the control of single organizations (such as the State of California's internal telephone system) to national or global public meta-networks such as America Online, AT&T Mail, CompuServe, MCI Mail, Prodigy, and Internet. While the telephone networks, and many private networks, include both hardware (the wires/fibers, communications satellites, microwave relay stations, switching centers, etc.) and the operating organizations, the meta-networks typically operate on top of the public switched networks. The public meta-networks typically offer a variety of services, from electronic mail to travel planning. For

---

[7] The *price* of telecommunications is not often directly related to the *cost* of delivery. Government regulation severely distorts the market in this respect, both at national and international levels. The price of trans-border information transmission, in particular, seems to be influenced—generally upward—by national policy, although the prices are beginning to come down.

telecommuting purposes, the electronic mail possibilities of these networks are probably the most compelling.

Local Area Networks

Local Area Networks are the main means for high-speed, intra-office telecommunications. LANs have grown from a rarity in the mid-1980s to the common means of communications among members of work groups who use personal computers. LANs communicate between personal computers at multi-million bits per second rates. However, the problem with LANs for telecommuting is embodied in their name: They are truly local in the geographic sense, while telecommuters are not.

The first step in solving this problem comes when one of the personal computers in a LAN acts as a telecommunications server. That is, it is connected to the network and, via one or more modems, to the telephone system. Telecommuters can dial in to the LAN communications server and get access to the files of their workgroup. Unfortunately, the telecommuters are limited in the rate of data transfer by the capacities of their modems; the fire hydrant-garden hose problem again. As the WANs go digital, however, this problem will diminish significantly.

Software

One of the means of reducing the demands on the physical transmission of all that data is through recognition that much of it is redundant. This is particularly the case for graphics. So, a variety of software packages have been developed, with more advanced ones continually appearing, that compress the data into much more reasonable lengths. So, what seems at first like a hideous problem, sending two million bits of screen information at the rate of seventy times per second, becomes much more tractable; only the changes from screenful to screenful are transmitted.

The result is that the conversion to digital transmission technologies promises to allow enormous expansion in the ability to transmit information between computers at low cost.

One of the most promising, if ill-defined, areas of software development is in what is known as *groupware*. Groupware's goal is to effectively interconnect work groups, regardless of the location of the individual group members. First evolving on

LANs, groupware usually migrates to WANs as well, allowing those connections to be global as well as local. The fundamental component of groupware is electronic mail, e-mail.

E-mail allows any member of the group to send messages to any other member, at any time. No big deal? Ah, but the point is that the recipient need not be at his computer when the message is sent; it will patiently wait until she shows up: The Death of Telephone Tag. Furthermore, the sender can require a receipt verification as part of the message, so that there is no question about whether the intended recipient got the message.

For example, I get many e-mail messages via Internet from researchers around the world. Typically, those messages are sent when I am not in the office. This saves not only time, but nerves. If a colleague in Indonesia were to phone me in mid-afternoon Jakarta time, I would not be ecstatic; it would be around 1:00 A.M. in California. Conversely, my calling her in mid-afternoon, PDT, might wake her from a sound sleep. The *asynchronous* nature of computer communications can be a significant asset to teleworking.

Facsimile works almost as well as e-mail, unless you want to keep the messages in digital form for further work or retransmission. This confinement to all-digital formats is particularly important when the group is jointly working on documents, spreadsheets or graphics. Conversion back and forth from analog (fax) to digital form can chew up huge amounts of time—as well as add to the paper storage problem.

Advanced groupware, such as Lotus Notes, includes the tools for many such types of interaction. The trend toward multi-media (another ambiguous term) for personal computers increases the likelihood that video conferencing will be almost a standard item on mid-cost personal computers in the late 1990s. Electronic white board software allows group participants to share drawings and sketches, hand-written notes, and other jottings, either live or asynchronously.

Note that the preceding has concentrated on interconnectivity software. One other aspect of software is important for telecommuting costs: duplication. Part-time telecommuters often have the same software at home—and/or on their personal computers at the telework center—as that on their personal computers in the principal office. Many, but not all, software manufacturers allow duplicate copies of their software to be kept on different machines, as long as no more than one copy is being used at a time. Other manufacturers insist on having separate licenses for each machine, regardless of the use patterns. This variance in software producer approaches causes severe hair tearing on the part of conscientious company information system managers. Hence, these usage rules will also evolve to a more standardized form (remember Rule Eight?) as telecommuting becomes an increasing presence in the work force.

In short, as new computer software becomes available for the traditional office, it will likely work as well in homes. Already, technology is not the problem for most telecommuters.

Security

One of the main concerns organizations have about distributed work situations like telecommuting is that company-private information may somehow get into the wrong hands or otherwise be compromised. This could happen either intentionally—the perpetrator is an employee who wants to damage the company—or unintentionally. As an example, a report in the trade magazine *PC Week*[8] discusses the claim that the annual disappearance rate of the notebook computers of a company's sales personnel is 8%. This is not believed to be the result of sheer carelessness; the sales people are very protective of the machines. Rather, the disappearances are imputed to competitors' attempts to get access to the company's main computers or to get the sales data that is stored in the notebook computers, or both.

The point is that sensitive company information is easiest to protect from outside intruders if it is kept securely locked in the company's vaulted, main office computers with no access allowed from the outside. This is true, but irrelevant in today's economic climate. It is not possible to totally exclude outside access to the data while operating in a teleworking environment, as most companies must. Telecommuters could be restricted to using only non-sensitive data while they are telecommuting but that would ultimately restrict the amount of telecommuting—and its benefits—available to employees.

Fortunately, there are some technological approaches to this problem, all of which act either to keep the information out of the hands of unauthorized people or to make it useless to them if they do get it.

---

[8] Jim Seymour's column, September 27, 1993, p. 85.

In a typical situation, the sensitive information is kept on the company mainframe or a LAN. The telecommuter accesses it by modem. Several layers of protection can be built in at this point, such as all or some combination of:

- having the telecommunications server not directly connected to the mainframe or LAN
- using "smart cards" that display a password that changes every 30 seconds or so, in synchronism with a password identifier in the computer being called (the telecommuter gets out a smart card, dials up the company machine, and enters the password appearing on the card at the moment)
- using a call back system—assuming all the password routines are completed correctly (many notebook computers have them built into the communications software, which is why they are desirable theft objects), the central computer dials the telecommuter's home or other prearranged phone number
- requiring a positive identification of the caller, such as a retinal scan or a fingerprint or hand shape detector

In cases where the sensitive information is stored on the telecommuter's computer, there are two (at least) other approaches to denying access to others. First, the sensitive information can be encrypted. Only the authorized telecommuter or others who know the key can decipher it. Quality encryption software is readily available.

Second, removable hard disks allow the information to be kept separate from the computer. Contemporary hard disks are small enough so that they are not bulky packages. Telecommuters can keep them locked up at home or carry them along as they travel between home, a telework center, and/or the principal office. This has other advantages, such as allowing easier sharing of computers in a telework office. Employee A at the local telework center usually has different software and data requirements than employee B who works at the same computer the following day. If both have removable hard disks, the problem goes away. The growth of the PCMCIA standard is allowing this option to be practical even if the hard disks ordinarily work on different machines.

Like many of the so-called technological barriers to telecommuting, security is not an impassable one. Nor need it be a particularly expensive barrier to overcome. Yet, any company that is considering—or practicing—telecommuting should put some serious thought into the realities of protection of its sensitive information.

Technology to Fit the Job

Given the general statements above, what do you really need to have in your own situation? Here are some sample setups for telecommuters in different types of jobs. The minimum requirements are based on Rule Six.

Routine Data/ Text Processing

Routine information jobs are often considered to be great candidates for telecommuting; the jobs are well-defined, as is the output, and it is relatively easy to check results. Most of these jobs are computer-intensive by now, or are on the verge of being computer-based. The key technology issues for telecommuting have to do with the means of raw input delivery/distribution and output retrieval. These are affected by the scale of the operation and the required turn-around times.

At the small workgroup scale, sneaker-net technology may suffice: the data/text processing person takes a stack of entry sheets or tapes home at night and comes in with a floppy disk or two after a day of telecommuting. At the next level of sophistication, the paper forms are sent by interoffice mail to the organization's facility that is nearest the telecommuter's home for daily pickup by the telecommuter, or dictation is downloaded to the telecommuter's answering machine. The results are sent by modem to a personal computer or LAN in the principal office. In any of these cases, the telecommuters can either be at home or in a telework center.

A key reason for failure of this simple situation is also simple: *forms fatigue*. As an example, a bank terminated a telesecretary program because of the forms hassle. The telesecretaries did indeed produce more accurate letters quicker, but the bank discovered that, because of the many different pre-printed forms it used, it had to employ another person at the headquarters printer to make sure the right form was in the printer when the data arrived from the telesecretary! Solution: Use printers (laser or ink-jet) and/or personal computer software that includes all the necessary form formatting information; the printer prints the form and the data simultaneously.

Massive order entry systems also are readily adaptable to tele-commuting. The most often quoted example is that of the J. C. Penney stores' phone entry operation in Milwaukee. In this case the necessary technology is a telephone distribution system that interconnects the main database functions to individual telecommuters' homes. Personal-computer-based telecommunications network distribution systems that cover this function are commercially available. SWIFNET, a system developed by Ambassador College to manage gift-giving resulting from their church's TV religious programs, is an example.

General Mid-Level Information Jobs

Many mid-level jobs are less dependent on technology than the routine jobs just discussed. Often, the only additional technology fix needed (aside from what most mid-level people already have at home, as in Figure 4-1) is some combination of an additional telephone line, pager, fax machine, and voice mail or answering machine. For many telemanagers, the primary task performed during telecommuting is catching up on reading and simple correspondence.[9]

The next step in technology escalation is the addition of a stand-alone personal computer. The primary use of the machine is for text processing, with occasional spreadsheet manipulation and preparation of graphics for presentation coming in second and third. Part-time telecommuters are more likely not to use computer telecommunications, preferring sneaker net—or laptop or notebook personal computers—as the primary means of information transfer. The work results are brought in to the principal office on the non-telecommuting days.

As the technology trends become more pronounced, the use of various forms of teleconferencing and/or groupware will spread. Since meetings occupy a substantial amount of the time of mid-level people, the fraction of time spent in non-face-to-face meetings will increase.

---

[9] By the way, as I forecast in the mid-70s, mid-level people using personal computers are increasingly performing tasks that once were reserved strictly for secretaries: text entry and editing. This is often decried as a waste of managers' more valuable time but that quibble is almost always wrong. The initial text entry process rarely slows down a manager or professional who is trying to get ideas out; most of the time is spent thinking up what to say next, even for inept keyboarders such as myself. When it comes to content editing, the idea originator is a far superior editor and time saver than the traditional mark-it-up, send-it-to-the-secretary-for-a-redraft, etc., process. All that is required is a fairly rudimentary knowledge of personal computer text processing software.

Specialists

The primary differences between specialists and other mid-level telecommuters are likely to be in the horsepower of their computers and/or software, and in the extent of their telecommunications usage. For example, actuaries are likely to need large amounts of data on either a mainframe or CD-ROM(s). Attorneys may need access to legal databases such as LEXIS. Architects and engineers may need CAD/CAM software and the highest-end personal computers. Programmers may need almost constant access to the mainframe, although possibly not during peak business hours. Information specialists need access to meta-databases such as DIALOG.

Sales and Field Service People

The appearance of laptop and notebook computers is revolutionizing sales and field service techniques in many industries. The prospect of instant access to all the critical information materially enhances the leverage of a sales call. Insurance salespeople can assemble and print policies on the client's premises. An insurance adjuster can complete the transaction in a single visit, using the hard-disk-stored database of replacement or repair costs. A realtor can display prospective homes in a client's own home; with advanced, three-dimensional CAD software, the realtor or an architect can even take the client for a virtual "stroll" through the building.

A telecommuting sales representative no longer needs a desk in the principal office. Lists of sales prospects can be downloaded to the representative's home. Final contracts can be printed either by the portable printer or, if a more visually attractive version is wanted, on the laser printer at home. Many large companies have noticed this possibility, in the past year or so, as a powerful means of reducing office space costs. But don't forget the security issues mentioned earlier.

Senior Executives

Senior executives are the most difficult to get out of an office. They tend to spend much more time in meetings, for the simple reason that they are hired primarily to deal with uncertainty and ambiguity—activities that generally require real face-to-face meetings. However, information technology acts to compress meeting time. A few years ago a senior executive of a large corporation told me that he typically used to spend a whole day discussing business problems at one of the regional facilities he visited. Now, with the ability to resolve a good portion of the routine matters by e-mail and telephone conferencing, the face-to-face aspects of the meetings were reduced to an hour or two. The new problem: what to do with the spare time at the regional centers?

Senior executives also tend to spend more time than average traveling, usually more time than they or their families would like. Like everything else noted above, the coming technological changes can allow the executives to substitute telecommunications for transportation for some of the meetings and change their "meeting" location to home from somewhere else.

Senior executives also tend to be significantly less willing to learn to use complex, user-surly software. If they are going to personally use a computer-with-software package, it had better actually be intuitive. Few contemporary systems can make that claim, although the executive gap is closing.

5

How Do You KNOW They're Working?

This leading question has a very simple answer: *You don't, not every minute!*

Not only that, but I'm pretty convinced that there really isn't a surefire way to *know* whether an information worker is actually working without getting inside his or her head—except in those cases where the work is apparent as physical activity of some sort, such as a secretary's keystrokes (he's not writing a letter home, is he?). Since much of information work is cerebral it is also invisible while it's going on. You can't see it. You can't hear it. You can't feel it.

Even if it's occurring—or failing to—before your very eyes.

So why do we managers have this compulsion about needing to be together with our employees in an office somewhere in order to do useful work? Perhaps it is because many of us have been brought up with the role model of the boss as cop. Those of us who adhere to this belief somehow feel that our personal charisma/charm/scowl will somehow inspire our workers into new heights of effort. A well placed glare or stroll past their desks from time to time will keep the laggards motivated. Therefore we have to be in the same location with them, *all* of the time, in order to get the best results. Otherwise the whole organization will run down in very short order.

There is a growing body of evidence, including our own measurements over the last two decades, that suggests that this isn't so, that the most vital attribute of a manager is leadership, not authoritarianism, not Big Brother behavior. I suggest that leadership can be practiced very well at a distance as well as up close. Telemanagement requires leadership ability. Leadership can be learned.

The Two Halves of Telemanagement

There are several key attributes of leadership. Two are particularly important for telecommuting. They are *trustworthiness* and *rapport*. The key to leadership is the ability to inspire others to empower themselves to work toward the same goals that the leader elucidates. Lack of leadership manifests itself by everyone in the group proceeding according to their own private goals and agendas, heedless of the group goals. Here is where trustworthiness and rapport come in.

Establishing Trust

The core virtue of quality telemanagement is trust. If you trust your employees to do their jobs, whether or not you are physically in their neighborhood, and they trust you to provide competent direction and guidance, reward them for work well done—and penalize them for work poorly performed, much of your job is under control. If you don't achieve that level of trust with everyone, then telecommuting is not recommended for those for whom the trust factor isn't there.

This is why it is generally easier to have well-established employees as telecommuters, rather than new workers. In fact, surveys of successful telecommuters generally show that they have been with their organizations longer than the average worker. These employees are known quantities. They know how the system works and their managers know how they work. Trust already has been established.

Yet, even in those cases, there may still be some nagging uncertainty. "I trust them to produce as long as they have the stimulation of the office environment, but what happens when they're at home (or in another, unknown quantity, telework office)?" Then we come back to the original issue. How do we arrange things so that we can build up the trust level to the point where we and our employees feel comfortable with it?

The following sections of this chapter treat those dilemmas.

Quality Communications

Trust depends on quality communication. Quality communication helps develop trust. "Quality" in this case refers to the idea that each party to a communication can accurately assess the meaning and intent of the other parties as a consequence of the communication. The law of uncertainty has been defeated, if only temporarily. This doesn't mean that you always *like* what the other person is saying, but it does mean that you *understand* it.

Our usual preconception is that the highest quality interpersonal communication occurs when we're face-to-face with the other person. We rely on a variety of cues—facial expression, body language, tone of voice, the physical surroundings—to help us interpret and expand on the information reaching us through speech alone. In telecommuting, at least for the next few years, those visual cues may not be available to us. We have to make do with a reduced palette of psychological colors to help us decide what the other person is *really* saying. This is one of the key factors that makes novice telemanagers nervous. They are concerned that the loss in communications richness will be so high that they will have severe difficulties in getting their ideas across to their employees, and in deciding what those employees are really doing.

Face-to-face situations also allow us to get a little lazy. Because our employees are there in front of us we can assure ourselves that, even though we may not know exactly what they're doing at the moment, we know that they're working, at least. Activity is reassuring. But possibly misleading. The real question is: Is all of that activity on our behalf? We depend on our personal charisma, enforced by periodic site visits (that is, management by walking around) to keep the troops in shape and ourselves well informed as to what's really going on.

I don't argue with the claim that face-to-face communication is *richer* than electronic substitutes such as telephones and electronic mail or computer conferencing. But face-to-face isn't necessarily *better* than these other forms in many situations. The key is in the content of the communications. After all, a short written communication can often be more meaningful than a twenty-minute meeting in which the real point never comes out, or is lost in a welter of extraneous comments and remarks.

One point to keep in mind is that you, as a manager, must make sure that the *frequency* of communications is such that the remote employees still feel themselves to be part of the gang at the office. "Out of sight, out of mind" can be a worry for them as well as for you. The delicate balance is between being in touch and being pestered, on the one hand and being forlorn on the other.

But the answer, of course, the real secret of much successful telecommuting communication is this: *Mix face-to-face and electronic communications so that the routine, information transmission types of messages get sent electronically and the very complex or emotion-related ones get sent or received face-to-face.* This is why most home-based telecommuters get into the office an average of two to three days a week. In all cases, the manager's job is to work on maximizing the effectiveness of all of the forms of communication. If the messages are getting through accurately, then we can start to rely on the self-motivational powers of each individual to get the job done. Occasional walking around doesn't hurt either.

Does this mean more work for the manager? In a sense, yes. It means more thought on how you and your employees communicate best and more action directed toward maintaining communications. But, if that work is done well, it means less work in unsnarling the communication foul-ups that can plague the best of offices at times.

The Buyer-Seller Mentality: Setting Performance Criteria

Although vital to the success of telecommuting, and of quality management in general, high trust and quality communications are fuzzy terms. Warm and fuzzy, maybe, but fuzzy nevertheless. The nexus of telecommuting management is the set of performance criteria that interconnect management and employees.

Focusing on Product Instead of Process

Any organization exists primarily to produce some kind of product; whether that product is widgets, groceries, laws, newspapers, inventions, regulations, or invoices. The product is what the organization's clients get and is the basis for their evaluation of the effectiveness of the organization. It makes no difference whether the organization is a separate entity, like a government agency or a company, or a subunit of a larger group, such as a section or department—the rule still applies. It makes no difference whether you are providing products and services to individual clients or analyses to other company work units—the rule still applies. The nature and quality of your product is what counts.

Furthermore, most constituents don't care *how* your product was developed. They *do* care about its quality—in terms of their own needs, its promptness, and cost. But how it was done and what processes were involved are not important to them.

In management we have a similar situation. Ideally, a manager should be able to give his or her employees a set of requirements for what they are to produce, establish the level of quality required, the cost in time and resources, the timing and rate at which the results are to appear, and leave it at that. Get out of their way. The employees skip back to their work places, produce the results as specified, and they all live happily ever after. Ideal organizations really do work like that. The ideal is the goal toward which we are striving.

Why is this so good? Because it is a situation in which there is minimum conflict, a minimum of working at cross-purposes, a maximum of all the pieces fitting well together: extremely low hassle for the manager—and the employees. Everyone knows his or her job, is competent and eager to produce results, and is able to adapt to the occasional schedule or cost or resource scarcity pressures that come along.

Back in the real world it appears that sometimes things don't work that way. Sometimes we don't specify the desired product adequately, *or* the employees don't have the skills, knowledge, or training to produce the results, *or* they didn't fully understand our specifications, *or* the needed resources just weren't available, *or* it took more effort than everyone thought, *or* . . . *or*, horrors, they are shiftless, lazy, and unmotivated, couldn't care less about getting the product out—and won't do it unless you stand over them like a warden and personally keep them at it.

If that last problem is *really* the case, you have significant trouble ahead. Fortunately, it's pretty rare, but certainly not impossible. Yet, we often act as if that *is* the case for many of our employees. It's time to examine why. *Are* they shiftless or is it that they aren't sure what they're supposed to do? *Are* they unmotivated or is it because they don't see where they are supposed to be going or why they should go there? *Are* they lazy

or just inadequately trained? Maybe what's needed is a better understanding—and agreement—on both sides as to what each part requires of the other. A pact or memorandum of understanding. Something that specifies what each of you will contribute to the common goal of getting that product out; that says it as unequivocally as possible (or as necessary). Then you have the basis for establishing that long term valuable: trust.

Your job is to provide specific, measurable, and attainable standards for the telecommuter to meet so that he or she knows what must be done, and when and how well it must be done.

When that is done consistently the relationship is simple: more trust means less contractual detail, less effort in negotiation, a smoother-running organization, less misspent effort on all sides, and probably a better-satisfied set of clients.

The Agreement Between Managers and . . .

Notice that all of this applies to work in general. It is not peculiar to telecommuting. But telecommuting relies much more heavily on the understanding or trust relationship simply because it is not practical for you to act as the cop or monitor for people who are somewhere else. If you have employees who you feel are just not trustworthy when they're out of sight, they should not be telecommuting—unless, of course, they work at a telework office. There someone else can see whether they look busy and you can check on their progress via periodic face-to-face meetings and more frequent phone calls or electronic messages. Your job should be as a coach and mentor, not an overseer.

By the way, all this talk about agreements and memoranda of understanding doesn't mean you have the prospect of a huge stack of legalistic documents in front of you. I mean it in the sense of a mutually binding agreement between you and one or more other parties. You are all free to change it mutually as circumstances change. The key word is *mutual*; all parties must agree on what is required of whom and when. The key concept is *attitude*. If you all believe you are in this venture together and you all share responsibility for the group effort, then you have most of it already. And it needn't be in writing. In fact, if you have managed your group for some time, most of this is probably understood already.

Employees

As a manager, your most important asset is your employees. I have spent considerable time on what is required of them. The agreement also must include what is required of you. Sometimes it's very little other than occasional guidance about some difficult aspects of their work. Other times you are required to provide much more: training, hand-holding through some new task, encouragement, access to scarce resources, special equipment. Whatever it is, make sure you *both* understand who is responsible for what. Do this with an agreement session as part of the initiation process for each new telecommuter, *before* he or she actually starts telecommuting.

It might also help to draw a schedule or flow chart showing when each side gets input from the other. In particular, try to schedule face-to-face meetings sufficiently far in advance so that your telecommuters can set up their home or telework or main office schedules. Make sure those meetings are productive, although this seems to happen naturally with telecommuters. You might also want to ensure that your employees are available during specific hours of the day so that you and others can communicate with them easily.

You may have lots of requirements for input that don't need meetings. Electronic mail, fax messages, and phone calls may satisfy most of those requirements. Other employees who come in to the office may act as couriers for written materials and supplies. Whatever the need, try to make it explicit *before* telecommuting begins.

This is also a good time to test the need for a group electronic bulletin board if your telecommuters are using personal computers. In short, make sure the agreement covers the communication resources you'll both need, as well as other resources including paper, forms, stamps, and sealing wax.

Others

Here the issue shifts in flavor more toward understanding than agreement. As a manager, part of your job is to let your colleagues, clients (both internal and external), and upper management know about the new working arrangements. It is important to get their feedback in order to tune your telecommuting operations successfully. Colleagues, clients, and upper managers all have their own expectations about what it is that your group is doing for, with or to them. Part of your task as a manager of telecommuters is to see that their most fond expectations are realized.

It might even be worth a test. Some time ago I came across a case where a senior manager of Company X remarked that he recently had found it much easier to get in touch with Employee Y because Y had installed an answering machine and promptly returned calls. Before, several hours or even days had elapsed in a classic case of telephone tag. The senior manager was astonished to hear that Y was now telecommuting from home, generally was out exercising in the early afternoon, and in mid-afternoon returned calls stored on the machine. Try it with some of your telecommuters—if the demands of your daily operations allow it.

Attitudes of colleagues are particularly important. Most members of organizations spend far more time communicating with colleagues than with superiors or subordinates. Those colleagues who are not telecommuting will invariably come up with comments like, "Well, did you come back from vacation just for this meeting?" Tensions like this will arise. The telecommuters are suddenly different. At first they are even more visible in the organization because of their difference. Therefore it is of extreme importance to let the non-telecommuters know that the telecommuters are still a vital part of the organization and are contributing at least as much as before to its progress. The trick is to let both sides know that neither of the groups—telecommuters and non-telecommuters—is specially privileged or specially burdened. The adjustment may take some time.

Meeting and Review Strategies

Why Have Meetings?

Why indeed? To share information. To find out what's going on. To gossip. To explore ideas, plans, and alternatives. To reacquaint ourselves with other people. To negotiate. To come to decisions. To politic. To cajole, exhort, persuade, threaten. To keep from getting our other work done. To relax. To be entertained. To feel important. To butter up to the boss. All sorts of reasons.

Telecommuting makes meetings more difficult, doesn't it? Certainly it's hard to have a spontaneous get-together if we're scattered all over the countryside. Telecommuters have to plan for meetings in advance so they can arrange to be there. More than one telecommuter has told us that this planning does have an interesting side effect: there are fewer meetings and those that do occur tend to be shorter and more productive. Let's examine what happens.

Formal Objectives

Most officially scheduled meetings have a formal agenda. Certain topics are to be discussed, decisions made, and subsequent actions taken by specific attendees. Ideally, the attendees come prepared to enter into those discussions, make those decisions, and take those actions. In very well run meetings, that is exactly what happens. That is what meetings are about. End of subject.

Sometimes.

Often (not in your case, of course, but in some other groups) meetings depart from the ideal somewhat. The agenda is less well defined, the participants are not always well prepared, the discussions tend to wander, and the decisions are not always made, are not well understood, or are a little too vague. It happens. When it does we can always have another meeting very soon to straighten out the ambiguities.

The problem with this is that in telecommuting situations togetherness-time is a valuable commodity, not to be wasted. Face-to-face meetings are more difficult to arrange because the travel time is way up; it's no longer the time it takes to walk from the office to the conference room. Meetings have to be scheduled, people have to show up and the formal content of each meeting must be dispatched expeditiously.

Hence, a few suggestions. Wherever possible, plan the meeting well ahead of time. Decide what must be discussed? What decisions have to be taken? Who should contribute? Are there alternatives if they can't make it? How much time should be spent discussing each item? To what extent are digressions permissible? Get the agenda together (including a statement of objectives), distribute it to the attendees in time for them to get prepared, and stick to it (within reason) at the meeting. This is what makes meetings shorter and more productive.

What can also make them productive for telecommuters is the use of electronic mail (for those organizations that have it) or fax transmissions to exchange information *before* the meeting. If all the basic information flow has already occurred, then the meeting itself can concentrate on the decision process rather than the information exchange which all too often makes up a large part of "normal" meetings.

Informal Objectives

Meetings also have informal, or at least not-formally-stated objectives, hidden agendas, or whatever euphemism is appropriate. The meeting serves as an occasion for A and B to get together on the side and make agreements about other topics than the formal ones of the meeting. Often the real—but unstated—purpose of the meeting is to establish pecking order or to gather support or test the water for something not on the agenda. One executive told us that she felt she could not telecommute because she had to attend the daily bull sessions (that were otherwise unproductive) just to maintain status in the organization. This, of course, is an admission that career advancement in that organization depends more on political than on objective performance factors. The success of telecommuting depends on the dominance of objective rather than political factors for career stability and advancement.

Thus it is important to examine these informal meeting objectives as an indicator of how well the organization can function in a telecommuting environment. If the informal objectives serve as sources of inspiration for improving output they are very useful. If they serve as foci for disruptive or inequitable coalition forming—degraders of teamwork—they can be counterproductive.

Scheduling Issues

Since most telecommuters will still need to be in an office part of the time, even though they may not be in the office an equal or greater amount of time, meeting scheduling will not be much more complicated. If you have regularly scheduled staff meetings it probably will be quite effective to continue to have them, unless they are daily affairs.

More problematic are the occasional or *ad hoc* meetings. These tend, by the laws of probability and the perversity of human nature, to be randomly distributed throughout the week. Hence, what starts out, with the best of good intentions, to be an effective home telecommuting schedule can soon degrade to an every-day-in-the-office-as-usual system. No gain. Remember, in the job screening process I concentrated on the ability to clump meetings as a perquisite to home telecommuting. It is therefore important to enforce that as much as possible.

The best way to do this is to regularize most meetings: staff, project review, brainstorming, planning, etc. Try to arrange them, or have the participants arrange them, so that none of the telecommuters needs to come to the office for meetings more than three days per week, on average. This does not necessarily mean that all the telecommuters come in the same days, unless they all go to the same meetings. It may be better, for facilities usage purposes, if the group's meetings can be staggered so that the entire group is almost never there at the same time. Make sure that each meeting chairperson distributes an agenda, either in person at a prior meeting, by memo, and/or by electronic mail or fax to the telecommuters, at least a day before the meeting.

This type of scheduling has some beneficial side effects, in our experience. First, meetings tend to be more effective as a consequence of prior, rather than ad hoc, agenda setting. Participants tend to be better prepared when they know they are discouraged from using the meeting as the occasion to "get up to speed" on the subject. Prior electronic messaging of information relevant to the meeting further serves this end. Conference room usage can be distributed more evenly, thereby cutting down on facilities needs.

The cost of this to you as a manager, or to the meeting chairpersons, is some extra time and effort spent in meeting planning. This can be more than repaid by the time released to you as a consequence of the shorter, more effective meetings that occur as a result. There are also some computer-based aids for all this, such as outliners (for agenda setting) and project scheduling packages.

All of the above is for relatively routine get-togethers. There is always the problem of the special occasions when an unexpected crisis (as contrasted to an expected crisis) occurs. Why is no one ever there when you want them? Here, there is clearly a problem with home, or maybe even local center, telecommuters. There is a necessary delay before they can get from wherever they are to wherever the meeting is to occur. The real question is: Do they really have to *be* there?

Telemeetings and Teleconferencing

Try holding some of these crisis meetings with tele-attendees via conference telephone. Note that audio teleconferences really require special equipment (that is, more sophisticated than a speaker-phone) and multiple phone lines *if* several people are involved. It's not absolutely necessary to have such equipment if such meetings are very infrequent, but it is important when telemeetings become regular events.

A telemeeting may be viewed mostly as a stopgap measure for including people in a conference who otherwise wouldn't be able to make it, as in our crisis meeting scenario. It may also be viewed as a great way of getting people together on other, more routine occasions; people who ordinarily wouldn't attend the meeting because of travel time pressures.

The latter motivation has been driving the growth of video and audio teleconferencing systems for the past decade. Video teleconferencing, in which TV pictures are sent between conference locations, is still relatively expensive, not to be used for the typical routine meeting in the typical office. However, audio conferencing can be a very useful tool for including everyone in a meeting without all of them actually having to go there. This use of telephone technology is not confined to regular telecommuters, of course. It can be used to augment many forms of meeting in traditional office situations.

Another form of electronic meeting is the computer conference, in which it's not even necessary that more than one person be "present" at the meeting at any given time. Computer conferencing is an expanded version of electronic mail: Each of the participants sends computer messages to one or all of the other participants over some period of time lasting from a few hours to months. The conference leader sets the agenda, keeps the discussions on track, organizes the summary of proceedings, and otherwise acts as the usual chairperson. The difference is that all of this is *asynchronous*; the participants "attend" when they have the time, which generally is not the same time that any one of the other participants can be involved. This is a particularly good tool when the participants are very widely separated geographically.

The Importance of Ongoing Feedback

Another area of good supervision that sometimes is taken for granted in telecommuting is the act of giving ongoing feedback about how the work is being done. Many employees—at all levels and in all locations—believe they don't get enough feedback about how they're doing; this is a special problem, though, for telecommuters who don't have as many opportunities to bump into the boss and get that feedback. That's why you have to take some extra effort to provide it.

That *extra effort* doesn't necessarily mean *extra work*. I'm talking about simple, quick, short ways of letting people know how well they're doing. This can include everything from a five-minute chat in the office when the person is in, to a brief message via electronic mail or voice mail, to a quick note you jot down in the margin of a memo or report you return to the employee. Keep it simple—and don't confuse this with the periodic performance appraisal.

Even though your telecommuters may be in the office three to four days a week, on average, don't wait for those times to give feedback. One way to keep them feeling tied in is to give each one a call or send an e-mail or fax message on the home days (for those so equipped). It can be very rewarding for a telecommuter to get a call saying, "Nice job!" when he or she has been working hard for several days on a big project. Better still, make that pat on the back public at a staff meeting.

Your department is probably not self-contained; your subordinates may have frequent interaction with customers, clients, or vendors as well as with others in your work unit. It is a good idea to get feedback from those people on occasion to get their views of your telecommuter's performance. You can funnel those comments back to the telecommuter, taking the place of some of the informal contacts he or she might have with those users in the office.

Informal Communications— The Key to Productivity

Most of the above has been concerned with formal communication within work groups. As we all know, there is a lot of communication in the office that does not occur in formal situations.

The Necessity for Informal Communications

This informal communication is absolutely necessary for the mental health of the organization. Meetings take care of the specific work objectives that must be met, set the marching orders for the members of the group, and form the backbone of the communications structure of the group. But those communications, vital as they are, are only part of the picture. Informal relationships between members of a group act as the glue that holds the group together. These relationships do much to establish the feelings of trust I keep harping on. They often serve as the means of surfacing danger signs and problems in the organization, or of spreading motivation, spirit, togetherness, or whatever you wish to call it, that transforms a collection of individuals into an interdependent, intersupportive team.

While formal communication can be packaged into memos, letters, reports, and meetings, informal communications are more elusive. Consequently, they are less easily captured by formal technologies such as computers. This is why I insist that, for most of us telecommuters, face-to-face get-togethers are absolutely necessary. We schedule meetings in the office ostensibly for formal communicating, but the hidden agenda is that a good deal of informal communication happens at the same time.

Keeping Telecommuters Linked into the Office

Nevertheless, telecommuters, whether at home or in a telework center, are potentially bereft of some chances for useful informal communication, compared with what is available in a traditional office setting. How can we compensate for or, even better, avoid that loss?

- Remember that the goal is to create the expectation of continued contact, and not to let them drift away from the mainstream.
- Don't assume anything about what you think the telecommuters might be hearing; take those extra few minutes to pick up the phone and pass along the word about changes in projects, organization, etc.
- Try to include the telecommuters in various social events around the office, especially the informal ones. If the gang is thinking of going out at lunch time or after work, try to do it on a day when the telecommuter is in the office—or do it so he or she can join you from home.
- Make it a point of routinely routing memos and other FYI items to the telecommuters; these don't always have to be sent to the home but should be waiting in the person's mailbox on days in the office.
- Remember that a big part of your role is as a "buffer" and problem-solver—make yourself available to provide any resources the telecommuter needs, such as manuals, supplies, answers to specific questions, etc.

This "linking" role is perhaps the only managerial duty in telecommuting that's not a part of your normal job. But it's one of the most important parts because it can make the difference between your telecommuters feeling isolated or still feeling like they're on the same team.

New Employees

One important question is whether to use new employees as telecommuters. For the most part, organizations with home telecommuters start with employees who have been with the organization for some time—at least long enough to learn the ropes of coping with the organization's system. In general this is the safest way to go. However, new employees may make perfectly fine home telecommuters from the start if the candidates:

- have been elsewhere in the organization for some time (that is, they may be new to you, but not to the organization);
- can be quickly trained to an adequate level of competency via telecommuting or by a short introductory course; or
- are not in jobs that require much detailed knowledge of organization policies and procedures (or if there aren't many policies and procedures).

If you use new employees as home telecommuters it is very important to get them to regular meetings at first and/or to make sure they get to "meet" their colleagues over the electronic network. New telework center employees, of course, have fewer problems in this respect. There the task is mostly to get them to meet the others at other centers and in the principal office over a relatively brief period.

Career Management for Telecommuters

Close behind isolation as a concern for telecommuters is one about their careers: Will they be "out of mind" because they're "out of sight"? Experience across many jobs and companies has not shown this to be true, but the concern may be there.

Here are some things you can do to put your telecommuters' minds at ease in this regard:

- **Highlighting:** Make sure the telecommuter gets the same credit or attention for the work done remotely as if it had been all done in the office. Sometimes this means you have take pains to put that person in the limelight so he or she may be gone but is not forgotten. Be careful that you don't draw too much attention, especially if it's out of proportion to the task. This can create a backlash among the in-office workers.
- **Job or Task Rotation:** Make sure the telecommuter doesn't get pigeonholed into doing only certain kinds of tasks because those are most easily managed from a distance. Again, the goal is to mirror the job or task mix that would have happened in the office. Task diversity builds skills and keeps the person from stagnating. This is, of course, true for all employees but a bit more relevant for telecommuters. This is also a way to ensure that the in-office employees don't feel that they are getting all the onerous tasks, while the

telecommuters are living it up at home; make sure that both telecommuters and non-telecommuters share in the less popular tasks.

- **Cross-Training:** A closely related aspect of career building is that of training several people, both telecommuters and non-telecommuters, to do some key tasks that are not necessarily part of their nominal jobs. This is particularly important in situations where clients, upper management, or other "outsiders" frequently call (or drop by) the principal office to get information on the projects in your unit. There should always be someone there who can "cover" for the distant telecommuter without strain. As is the case for job rotation, this expands everyone's horizons.

- **Even-Handed Appraisal:** When it comes time for performance appraisals, make sure you realize that telecommuters may use new methods to do old tasks. They sometimes do this to cope with (or take advantage of) their relative independence. Don't penalize them for using new means to get to the same or better ends as before. In fact, their different ways of performing their work may be worth exporting to your other employees. Don't forget: It's the results that count for both the telecommuters and the non-telecommuters.

Spotting Problems Early

Despite all the training and everyone's best efforts, it's still possible for snags to develop. Telecommuters can run into problems affecting their performance or satisfaction. Your job is to watch for some early signs and act on them quickly. Here are some of the obvious and not-so-obvious "red flags":

- Job performance starts to suffer (either in quantity or quality of results).
- Absenteeism starts to increase.
- You, or the telecommuter's co-workers start having communication problems—either decreased or poorer communication.
- The telecommuter shows less interest in attending department meetings or otherwise shows signs of becoming a "loner." (Don't confuse this with signs of irritation at ill-organized and rambling meetings. Telecommuters tend to

become more time-conscious and agenda-oriented as they gain experience.)

If you see these or other signs, don't jump to conclusions that the person is necessarily having serious problems. After you've verified your observations—and are certain that something has changed for the worse—your first step is to get more information.

The best first step is to confront the problem with the telecommuter—share your observation as factually as possible, and then ask for his or her comments. Your goal here is to have an open discussion that will lead to a clear understanding of the problem, and a joint commitment to resolving it.

A little bit of empathy goes a long way here. The telecommuter might be having problems adjusting to the new routine, or could still be trying to work out the fine points of scheduling her or his time. Sometimes, the relative independence that telecommuters have can be overwhelming, and some more detailed supervision can help.

In summary, you want to get an open discussion going and keep it going until both of you are comfortable with the outcome. Don't assume the telecommuter must return to the office full-time, though that's certainly an option. In most cases, that's the *last* resort, not the first.

6

Making it Happen: Planning, Development, and Training

In order to begin a formal telecommuting program it is necessary to convince a number of key people that telecommuting is worth trying. In order to do that, you probably need to have a well-organized and well-thought out plan. Once you have accomplished those tasks, the next step is to select and train the telemanagers and telecommuters. Neither the ability to be an effective telecommuter, nor the fundamental understanding that telecommuting may be a better way of doing business, springs fully formed into a person's brain at birth. Yet the principles and disciplines of telecommuting are relatively easily learned through a combination of planning, communication, and training techniques, discussed next.

The Preliminaries

Any organization with more than a few employees has some sort of decision structure and a set of individuals who make the key decisions. Because telecommuting is a new concept to many, and because reluctance to change does appear to be a common trait among managers, it is very important that the new telecommuting program get the support of these key decision makers.

**Convincing the
Head Shed**

Not everyone in the decision structure has to agree that telecommuting is the greatest thing since the invention of the wheel. But the chief executive officer (and/or chief operating officer) and all of the chain of command down the line to each and every prospective telecommuters should be at least neutral to the concept. The CEO should be positively behind it—or at least willing to try it for a suitable period. Therefore, your first step in mounting a telecommuting program is to convince the members of the executive suite that it's worth trying.

The fundamental job of every CEO is to ensure the organization's economic viability. Therefore, a presentation aimed at that aspect is the most likely to get the CEO's positive attention. The CEO needs to be presented with a set of cogent, quantitative reasons why the organization should expend any resources to develop telecommuting, as well as a convincing plan for making it happen. Chapter 1 contains the most common basic arguments. Your job as a telecommuting instigator is to particularize those arguments to your organization; to emphasize the issues that are of most concern to your CEO.

Almost always, the key economic issues are some combination of these top four:

- Maintaining or increasing productivity
- Decreasing office space needs
- Attracting or retaining critical skills among the staff
- Complying with air quality or other environmental regulations

That is, increasing output at the same or lower costs.

As an erstwhile presidential candidate was so fond of saying: Here's the deal. Convert those four issues (or as many of them as you think the CEO worries about) into numbers.

- What's the average salary (plus fringe benefits?) of your potential telecommuters? What's the annual dollar impact of a 12% improvement in their productivity?[1]

---

[1] Our data indicate effectiveness changes ranging from 0% to 300%, with averages from 10% to 20% or more *as estimated by direct supervisors*. There is also some correlation between salary and productivity improvement. That is, higher paid employees tend to get a larger productivity boost from telecommuting than do entry level workers. However, I would not bet the store on this relationship.

- What's the annual cost of your office space? What if you could eliminate the need for one-third of it for your telecommuters?[2] [Or, for telework centers, what's the differential between the costs of headquarters office space and the space at the local telework centers?]
- What does it cost to replace one of your potential telecommuters? Figure a year's salary for each replacement[3] in other than very easily replaceable jobs. Turnover rates for telecommuters tend to be near-zero. What's the usual rate for your organization?
- What's the tab for failing to meet your local air quality regulations? In Southern California, it can be as high as $25,000 for every day of non-compliance!

You also have to think about the costs of getting these benefits. Figure on spending about 5% of the telecommuters' salaries for the job of starting the program, acquiring some extra equipment and/or software, training the telecommuters and telemanagers, and evaluating the results for at least a year. The *net* benefits (that is, benefits minus costs) to the organization, for properly managed telecommuting programs with mid-level participants, should be on the order of $8,000 or more annually *per telecommuter* (in 1993 dollars). That is what we have found in several programs in both the private and public sectors. That figure does not include any benefits to either the telecommuters, their families, or the community at large.

The Plan

Rather than say: "Just do it," the boss is likely to ask for a more fully developed plan than can be delivered in a twenty-minute briefing. In a sense, this book contains the elements of a project plan. What remains for you to do is to particularize it for your organization. Make sure it answers the main what, why, where, who, how, and when questions. Put in the names of the potential participating groups. Develop an implementation schedule, together with a description of what has to be done. Assess the

---

[2] Be careful about this one if your CEO has just spent the last five years convincing the board that the company should move into new quarters, at the cost of several megabucks.

[3] That includes the loss of the services of the person while the replacement is being found; the costs of finding the replacement; the diminished productivity of those who are filling in for, or depending on the services of, the departee; and the diminished productivity of the replacement until s/he gets up to speed in the organization.

operating costs of the project. Estimate the potential benefits for each participating group (what's in it for them?).

At this stage it is often useful to develop a steering committee comprising senior decision makers from the most-likely-to-participate organizational units. The purpose of the committee is twofold: to give you good advice on successful implementation and to have those key opinion leaders buy into the program. That is, the plan resulting from this effort is a marketing plan as well as an implementation plan. The thoroughness and scope of this plan is what may finally convince the boss to go ahead.

As to schedule, if your organization is small (that is, the CEO knows everyone personally), then this may take only a day or two. If your organization has thousands of employees, figure that it may take several months to convince the rest of the organization's managers to participate, two months or more to get all the telecommuters trained, and at least a year of evaluation and follow-up training to get to the point where the operational issues and procedures have been thoroughly tested. Clearly, some of these schedule numbers depend on the size and complexity of your organization.

If the CEO doesn't buy the project at this point, you have a problem. If you can, find out what objections still exist. See if you can mount compelling arguments to overcome them. The most common objections tend to be of the "I have too many more pressing worries on my plate" variety. Good. See how telecommuting can address each of them. Let's face it: If increasing profitability and smoother sailing won't help your organization, it's time to begin looking for other career opportunities.

The Rest of the Hierarchy: Orientation Briefings

Once the boss is convinced, it is time to develop the rest of the chain. We always adopt a strict rule of volunteerism for telecommuting programs: *If manager X does not want to participate, then neither X nor any of X's subordinates are to participate.* The reason for this is very simple: People can become incredibly ingenious at defeating a system that they don't like. Therefore, either convince them that they are going to like it or leave them alone. Most organizations have a treelike reporting structure. The volunteer rule simply lops some of the branches and twigs from your opportunity tree.

However, X and all other managers should be given the chance to participate—as well as an informative orientation briefing as to why they should want to be involved. This briefing[4] should be similar to the one given to the CEO, although possibly with the detailed numbers presented for their level of the organization rather than (or in addition to) the numbers for the organization overall.

In fact, the first of these briefings to upper-mid management should be by or with the chief executive officer or another key individual whose support is crucial for the long-term success of the program. The department or division chief might hold a general briefing so that employees understand the program from management's point of view. Opportunity for questions should be provided. Usually the questions deal with the details of telecommuting operations. This is a good opportunity to explain the TeleGuide in Chapter 7, or your own version of it.

THiS PLAN WOULD CONVINCE GOD TO TELECOMMUTE!

YEAH, BUT WiLL THE BOSS BUY iT?

After each briefing, ask the assembled managers to volunteer themselves and their subordinates as potential participants in the project. Some organizations—and their subunits—may opt out of the project at this point. Make sure those managers realize that, when the demonstration project[5] is deemed to be a success and telecommuting is extended to the whole organization, they will have missed out on a year or two of vital experience.

Finally, brief the prospective telecommuters in the organizational units that have decided to stick with the plan. These people are your first volunteers and, most of them, trainees.

At this stage it is time to use the procedures outlined in Chapter 2 to make up the final list of trainees. Unless your organization is incredibly tightly organized, you will find that the steps up to this point will be reiterated several times as managers in your organization have second thoughts. (Gee, maybe I'd better check this out after all!) This is what tends to make the training phase of the project last several times longer than your most conservative initial estimate.[6]

---

[4] Or these briefings. If your organization has several hierarchical levels, it may be necessary to give briefing to each level in turn.

[5] Don't call it a pilot project (as I have done). Apparently, *pilot* connotes: "after it's over we can forget about it;" while *demonstration* seems to mean: "they're serious about this and the purpose of the project is just to work out the bugs."

[6] My personal record, so far, is a "one-month" training series that has extended over more than 15 months as more managers changed their minds.

TeleXer Training Issues

The importance of proper training of telecommuters, telemanagers and of those non-telecommuters with whom they deal regularly cannot be overstressed. Employees and managers alike may be intimidated by the concept, nontelecommuting colleagues may have misapprehensions about the nature of telecommuting, families need to understand the changing roles of home telecommuters, and the work patterns of the telecommuters themselves tend to change. It is extremely important to provide pre-implementation and during-implementation training (and assessment) for all of those who are directly affected by telecommuting.

Central to the training plan is the identification of the differences between traditional work situations and those of telecommuting. For example, techniques of supervision (as discussed in Chapter 5) are likely to be different, as are performance indicators. Employees with limited or no prior computer experience will need familiarization training as well as a readily available "hot line" source of advice during work if they will be using computers as telecommuters. Home telecommuters may need training or advice on how to work with their families to eliminate distractions during working periods.[7] The nature and details of the types of training required will depend on the types of work and work situations of the prospective telecommuters.

Telecommuting by large numbers of employees may be a novel concept but it is not a work style without precedents. Many employees of large organizations already work remotely from organization or district headquarters: forest rangers, detectives, construction managers, sales personnel, and field engineers all work "off site" with varying degrees of contact with their supervisors. For those workers and their managers the training to work independently and to monitor from a distance are already ingrained in the system. To achieve the same level of confidence regarding telecommuting requires attention to:

• how each participating work unit functions now and

---

[7] Actually, my experience has been that, in our contemporary world of two-earner households, there is fairly little interaction with the rest of the family for many telecommuters. This is because the non-telecommuting earner is usually at work somewhere else. This will change as the number of two-telecommuter households increases.

- what training and procedures (in addition to those for the new technology) will optimize productive functioning in the future.

Training What?

How do you know how much training is required? We recommend that you develop this information by means of the survey of potential telecommuters described earlier. One of the products of the survey should be an estimate of the extent and nature of the changes facing individual telecommuters, their managers and their peer groups. This estimate will serve to scope the types and nature of training that might be required.

The Book(s)

As one part of the training approach, we feel that it is important to have an easily readable book for telecommuters that can serve as a valuable aid and reference during the acclimatization process. This book was designed with that thought in mind, although it may be "overkill" for some telecommuters.

It is also desirable to have the participating telecommuters and telemanagers develop a company-specific addendum to the book as their experience with telecommuting progresses. Although the book you are reading at this moment can act as core material, specific additional anecdotes and rules appropriate to your organization may make it more personal and positive as a learning tool.

Training Face-to-Face

In addition to such written aids, it is important to have face-to-face training sessions with the prospective telecommuters both prior to the initiation of their new work styles (and after the orientation briefings mentioned earlier) and at intervals throughout the start-up phase. In the latter case, for example, focus group sessions, or the formation of "users' groups" can serve as excellent means of self-training and maintaining group communications.

The active participation of some prospective telecommuters can materially aid the training plan. You can help employees identify their own training needs and requirements, through meetings and telephone interviews during the initial period of implementation, and during or shortly after the participant selection process. Thus, the training plan, as well as other key parts of the implementation plan, will be guided by those who are or will be the ultimate recipients of the training. Then, when the actual personnel training begins, the training aids will be optimally matched to the requirements of the participants.

The following sections describe the issues and approaches in more detail.

Training Topics and Methods

The most extensive training requirement is for those telecommuters who will be working at home. In many cases, particularly among professionals and those individuals who are accustomed to working independently, very little extra training may be required. For some individuals, such as those who are used to working under detailed supervision, fairly extensive training may be in order.

Learning to Work in the Home

Objectives of Training for Off-site Work. Learning to work at home requires developing or adopting self-supplied cues to "go to work," continue, and stop working. At the office, group behavior, whether or not it is formally imposed, sets times to start and stop work within "allowable" variances, exercises a peer pressure to keep working, and provides a hierarchical supervisory structure that sets productivity standards and maintains the group routine.

When an individual travels for business, work periods are structured by scheduled appointments, flight departure times, and the group behavior at each place she or he conducts business.

During overtime work periods, the task overload which necessitates the extra work time tends to be stimulus enough to continue working even if one is alone and without direct supervision.

In telecommuting situations, however, either an externally imposed structure or self-imposed artifices may be required to maintain discipline equivalent to what one has in the office.

Employees beginning to telecommute from home may need training in the following areas:

Scheduling Work Periods. Most home telecommuters work on schedules that are either evolved to fit their individual preferences and household constraints or are determined by the nature of the job. Programmers, for example, tend to work late at night during hours when response times are fastest on mainframe computers. Most people work by the clock, but not necessarily by the same time periods as for on-site work.[8]

A common change is *schedule chunking*: from the traditional nine-hour continuous day[9] (with lunch in the middle), to two or more chunks of two to four hours, only some of which are during conventional office hours. As another variation, some telecommuters change to a more flexible twenty-four-hour day, seven-day week of interspersed work and leisure. If interaction with on-site peers is required as part of the tasks performed at home, those work hours may need to be synchronized. Where use of electronic- or voice-mail satisfies the work communications needs, the time periods worked at home need not overlap on-site work hours.

Accepting Shifts in Household Responsibilities. A worker coming home to work, even for intermittent periods, must be prepared for his or her new role within a shared habitat. Assuming traditional role models, "he" must be prepared to meet expectations that now he is home he can do certain chores and "she" must be prepared to give up household territory (aural as well as physical). Persons who successfully home telecommute find that, although the trade-offs of being at home are positive, there may be adjustments to be made.

Controlling Interruptions. This is probably the most difficult adjustment home-based telecommuters may have to make. Establishing an office environment in a house that "has a life of its own" requires setting new precedents for which interruptions are permissible and which are not. Most telecommuters cannot isolate themselves totally within the household. They and their families can mutually agree, however, that the family exchanges

---

[8] Several telecommuters list the main virtue of telecommuting as its *metabolism equalizer* nature. It allows them to work during their most energetic periods– that are not consistent with normal office hours.

[9] Many telecommuters also work on compressed schedules such as 9-80 (8 nine-hour-plus-lunch days and 1 eight-hour-plus-lunch day in two weeks) or 4-10 (4 ten-hour-plus-lunch days per week). The same principles apply here. However, managers are even more reluctant to accept telecommuting for compressed-week employees, arguing that they are already spending diminished time in the office. Our data indicate that the benefits of telecommuting are relatively insensitive to these different schedule options; they work for all of them.

routinely will take place during times set for breaks so that home workers are not continually distracted from their jobs.

Even having trained all members of the household, including himself or herself, the telecommuter must take some interruptions in his stride. Stopping to answer the delivery person's knock on the door may be no more distracting than a co-worker's interruption unless one is fighting a grievance over spousal responsibilities. Frequently, these "interruptions" are themselves useful for relaxation and posture realignment breaks, particularly as a means of dragging telecommuters away from their computers.

Resisting Temptations. When does freedom become license? With all those on-site restrictions lifted, it's an opportunity for bad habits to take over. Snacking, drug abuse, watching a TV soap opera, and other temptations lurk just around the corner. *Impulse-stifling* is another key arrow in the experienced telecommuter's quiver.

The most effective approach for this aspect of working at home is to heighten the telecommuter's awareness that such problems often arise and to suggest immediate counteractivities, such as relaxation techniques, development of positive rewards for not succumbing, avoiding the source of temptation (for example, not working in the kitchen), and developing strict break schedules. If lecture style techniques have insufficient impact, then group discussions with fellow victims of temptation may work.

For several years we have taken informal polls of the net weight gain or loss of home-based telecommuters as a measure of the TTD (Tele-Temptation Differential). The answers are still inconclusive; weight losses are reported about as often as gains. At home, the refrigerator may be too close. At the office there are the birthday, going-away, and any-other-excuse parties, not to mention the doughnuts in the morning.

Training Methods

In a telecommuting program of any size it is not possible to train everyone on a one-on-one basis. Group sessions are inevitable. Our practice has been to hold initial training sessions with telecommuters separately from the manager sessions. A typical session should have from fifteen to twenty-five participants. Fifteen is used as a lower target figure because you would like to have enough interaction among the participants to stimulate discussion—smaller groups will often just sit there. The upper limit is suggested in order to keep the interaction from getting out of hand. These numbers apply to the final initial training sessions, completed after the orientation briefings have been given.

The purpose of these sessions, which are generally in a traditional lecture format, is to provide practical applications—how-to ideas—for home telecommuters to show them how to organize their work and to set up a home office. In the latter case, you might include a slide show of sample offices plus descriptions of the techniques for deciding what equipment is needed and where it should be placed, space selection, and related issues. However, we have found that most telecommuters at the professional or mid-level management level already have offices established at home. Therefore, as in most of these training topics, it is a good idea to test the pre-existing level of expertise of your audience before boring them with information they already have.

After the general how-do-we-do-it sessions, (one for managers, one for telecommuters) each of which typically will last from two to three hours, a third session is required. In this session, the telecommuters and their direct supervisors meet to establish mutual expectations and agreement on the guidelines for remote work. We anticipate that within your organization's overall policies there is a reasonable amount of flexibility in the working agreement between a supervisor and a given employee. The details of how and when work is to be performed will be first, task-related, and second, dependent upon individual home circumstances. This session need not be a formal one as long as the supervisor-telecommuter groups engage in the session *before* telecommuting begins.

I have found that follow-up workshops or focus group sessions are invaluable both as a neutral forum in which to share successes and resolve problems and as a vehicle for reinforcing the messages of the initial training. These should be held at decreasing intervals after telecommuting has begun. The first ones should be within a few weeks of the initial training sessions.

Employees also may need access to a "guru" for technical help and to an ombudsman, a peer network, and co-worker groups for work-related counsel.

Telemanagement Topics

Management of Home Telecommuters. A major incentive for employees to work in their homes is the opportunity to set up a more flexible schedule of work and personal activities. From the management viewpoint one consequence of that work mode is that the worker can no longer feasibly be monitored by time. The time the employee arrives and remains more or less in view has been a measure of performance for many managers. A supervisor who permits employees to work remotely *must adopt the management style of monitoring by results instead of by process.* He or she must set a completion time and level of quality for a given task and send the employee off to do that job. Not every supervisor now has the management style that supports remote work. Not every manager will want to employ that style.

Topics that pertain specifically to monitoring remote employees include the following:

Setting Performance Standards. "It is extremely rare to find any valid or validated standard of performance on any level. Some units may have some fragmentary standards and some directors may think they have them [but don't]."[10] It is better not to attempt a universal performance measure per se because it is likely that most situations will contain numerous exceptions to the "rule."

Although generalized performance standards may be lacking, any manager usually has in mind a level of expectation for each employee under his or her supervision. Many projects have an historic background on which to base person-hour estimates. Thus work can be assigned with some confidence as to the timeliness and level of quality with which it will be delivered. With the same degree of predictability, the manager can assign a task to be performed at home.

There is a major difference which requires training to overcome: The telecommuter and supervisor must comprehend the verbal understanding to which they are jointly agreeing. For example, they could reach agreement on milestones. *The worker must accept responsibility for accomplishing the project, but the manager must ensure that the desired results and milestones are clearly and fully stated.*

---

[10] A comment by one of the telemanagers we have trained.

Communicating with Remote Workers. Managers find that they must be more aware of how they communicate to personnel who telecommute. Instructions must be more complete when they cannot be continually amended. Thus, vaguely stated requests are less easily upgraded to specific requirements when the manager is no longer "looking over the shoulder" of the task in progress.

Managers become more skilled in giving directions because they are forced to define to themselves what it is they want accomplished. This differs from saying, in effect, to an employee "I'll know what I want when I see it."

Training in communication skills must focus on (1) task definition and (2) performance expectations.

Setting Guidelines for Remote Work. The process of setting guidelines for working at home must involve coming to a mutual understanding between supervisor and employee. Each case will be unique, since the major benefit for the employee is a work mode that fits each one's individual situation. The agreement can be formalized, however. One of the objectives of the demonstration project is to set up model formal agreements.

Troubleshooting. Training for managers of remote employees must include techniques for dealing with below-standard performance. Role playing might be an effective way to practice differentiating between "excuses" and valid reasons for non-performance. As a last resort, the manager can bring the employee back on site to work. But particularly during the demonstration project focus should be kept on finding the solutions that make telecommuting beneficial to both manager and employee.

Self-Identification of Management Styles. The first step in defining a training program appropriate for a given manager is to identify her or his current management style.

The offices responsible for management training in departments have developed management training programs. Validated instruments are available for supervisors to identify their own management styles. Those should serve very well as the first step in screening candidate supervisors for the telecommuting demonstration.

7

Rules and Regulations

It is important to have a core set of rules and regulations for telecommuting, whether it is a demonstration project or everyday standard operation. The rules should be sufficiently specific to minimize the risk of ineffective performance but sufficiently flexible to allow tailoring for work unit and individual cases. The following are key issues that should be covered by the formal rules.

Key Issues

Allocation of Responsibility

Emphasizing who is responsible for what, such as defining explicitly what is to be done, doing it, and providing help, advice, supplies, maintenance, etc., is of critical importance. Also important is the home telecommuter's responsibility for keeping the home office in OSHA-acceptable condition.

Fair Employment Practices

Telecommuters should *not* be special people in terms of the company rewards system. Telecommuter qualification criteria should be as objective as possible, based on performance criteria. There are no other restrictions.

For example, your telecommuters should *not* be working on a piecework basis. They should not fear loss of income resulting from an irregular supply of work. We assume that participant telecommuters will form agreements that will afford them a steady supply of work and that they will not be susceptible to income fluctuations like those who labor on a piecework basis. In addition, participants need not fear onerous work speed-ups (that is, an escalation of minimum requirements to turn the home office into the electronic sweat shop conditions feared by labor organizations).

However, although the baseline employment requirements should remain as established by general agreement with all company workers, we expect that telecommuters will realize productivity increases sufficient to offset any additional net cost of implementing a telecommuting program. (This "net cost" should be calculated as total additional costs incurred by the company in equipment purchases, designation or provision of new telecommunication lines, et cetera, minus company savings in office space rental and maintenance, parking lot leases, et cetera.)

In a survey we performed in the mid-1980s, we found that about 80% of mid-level information workers[1] worked at home *in addition to* their daily stint at the office. Telecommuting should not be just another way to get employees to put in extra hours after their office-based work day. Work assignments should be established clearly prior to implementation. We recommend that these agreements not be made subject to rising expectations. That is, the contractual agreement should specify that implementation of this work style shall not be a means of securing computer-mediated overtime, but that telecommuting will take place as substitution for more "traditional" working arrangements.

Time Accounting

This appears to be an issue primarily for home telecommuters. How are they to account for hours spent, if at all? Honor system (recommended); the boss drives by every three hours; monitors the telephone or ?? Whatever the details, there should be an agreement *before telecommuting begins* as to what the rules are. The issue may also exist for telework center telecommuters in cases where there is no on-site supervisor to take attendance.

---

[1] The survey involved about 1,000 mid-level workers in a number of Fortune 100 firms. More than 3% of the workers responded that they spent at least 8 hours per week telecommuting; that is, without going in to their principal office. At the time, none of these firms had a formal telecommuting program.

However, although it may be important to think about how long it will take to do a specific task—as a means of estimating effort, your ultimate focus should always be on the results. Was the task performed as expected, and in time for the pre-established deadline? If so, fine; that performance result, not the time spent arriving at it, should be the success criterion. Time spent is primarily useful for estimating how long it will take to get the next similar result. For information work of even moderate complexity, time accounting is at best an uncertain performance measure.

Sick Leave

As above. If you're sick, you're sick. But remember that what once caused use of sick leave, such as attending the kid's school play in the afternoon, can disappear as the home telecommuter makes it up early that morning or that evening.

Liability and Insurance

Who's responsible when the home telecommuter trips over the cat in the den at three A.M.—on the way to register that great, dream-induced idea—and breaks a leg? Who's responsible for

theft of a computer owned by the company from an employee's home? Who's responsible for paying the insurance premiums?

Most successful telecommuting organizations have accepted the premise that the home telecommuter's office is covered by the same rules as the principal office. Job-related injuries are job-related injuries, regardless of the location of occurrence in this view. However, this theory has not yet been tested as far as we know. In any case, employees should be given clear and adequate information as to the need to document claims as well as the documentation procedures.

Putting It Together

We address these issues explicitly here in the form of a set of guidelines for a telecommuting demonstration project, governing the relationships between the company and the telecommuters. The guidelines are collected in a document called "The TeleGuide." The TeleGuide covers most of the items of contention that have arisen in past telecommuting experiments, as well as addressing potential problems that have not yet arisen. Each employer tends to put a slightly different structure on the guidelines. Therefore, these should be used as a starting point for your own, customized set.

The first step, as an integral part of the program planning process, is to review the TeleGuide and then submit them to the legal staff—with a specific deadline for comments.[2]

After completion of the legal review, your version of the TeleGuide should be sent to senior executives and distributed as part of the training documentation. To ensure that the senior executive doesn't get relegated to the bottom of the In stack, you may want to have the TeleGuide accompanied by a cover letter signed by the CEO. The version for the training sessions may either be incorporated with other materials or serve as a separate document. In the latter case, you may also wish to attach the CEO cover letter, or one from a more immediate manager.

The "we"s in the TeleGuide refer to these managers. These guidelines should be accompanied by an agreement like that described earlier for home telecommuters. There should also be a signature page on which the prospective telecommuter attests that he or she has read and understood the guidelines. A

---

[2] Attorneys love to agonize over every word in the guidelines, so make sure that the legal staff realizes that timeliness is a virtue. This is likely to be a more persuasive argument if the attorneys are also in line to be telecommuters.

telecommuter's acknowledgment, a supervisor's checklist, an outline of possible department-specific rules, and an outline of a detailed work agreement follow the guidelines.

TeleGuide: An Introduction to Telecommuting

This guide covers the relationships between the Company and the participants in the Company Telecommuting Demonstration Project. It describes telecommuting and the general rules of participation. These rules are effective for the duration of the employee's telecommuting or the duration of the project, whichever is shorter.

The purpose of the TeleGuide is to answer common questions about the Company's demonstration telecommuting project and is for informational purposes only.

Participation in the demonstration project is voluntary and, therefore, management retains the right to determine the job characteristics best suited for telecommuting participation. Moreover, the selection process, as well as the decision to send a participant back to his or her regular work environment, is the sole responsibility of management.

What Is Telecommuting?

Telecommuting is the substitution of telecommunications and/or computers for commuting to work. There are two main forms of telecommuting: home telecommuting and telework center telecommuting. In home telecommuting, a Company employee works at home instead of in the office, possibly with the aid of a personal computer. In telework center telecommuting, the employee works at an office that is close to his or her home rather than at his or her regular location. Telecommunications systems interconnect the home telecommuters, the telework centers and the "principal" offices so that everyone can keep in touch.

Why is the Company interested?
For several reasons. *First*, if telecommuting becomes widespread it could have major positive effects on traffic flow and air quality. *Second*, telecommuting may reduce costs and increase effectiveness. *Third*, telecommuting may beneficially alter energy use, the general quality-of-life, and the economy.

Why should I be interested?

If you want to reduce the time you spend commuting, arrange your working hours to more closely fit your off-work plans, feel more in charge of your life and your job, get closer to your family, or reduce some of your work-related expenses, then maybe telecommuting is worth a try. There is no guarantee that all—or even some—of these things will happen for you, but those are among the reasons most often given by telecommuters for their enthusiasm.

The Company Telecommuting Demonstration Project

The Company Telecommuting Demonstration Project is designed to test the desirability of telecommuting for the Company and for Company employees. Other tests of telecommuting in business and government over the past fifteen years have shown that employee job satisfaction generally increases, as does effectiveness. Both the employee and the employer are winners in this situation. The Company is testing telecommuting to develop methods for ensuring that both employees and management achieve positive and satisfying results; then the use of telecommuting can be appropriately expanded throughout the Company.

What's going to happen?

The project is in five main parts. The first part comprises orientation briefings for potential telecommuters and their supervisors. Part two focuses on deciding who will be the participating telecommuters. Part three includes training for telecommuters and their supervisors. The fourth part starts when the first project telecommuter begins telecommuting. It will last at least twelve months after telecommuting first officially starts. Finally, part five consists of the evaluation of the project. It will result in recommendations to the chief executive officer concerning expansion of telecommuting.

Why have a special project; why not just do it?

Because telecommuting is a departure from traditional ways of working. It is important to make sure that it is done right. It is not advisable to rely on undocumented or overblown tales of great success or miserable failures, either in Company departments or other organizations. Where telecommuting succeeds it is important to know exactly why—and how much. More importantly, in cases where it doesn't work out we want to know how to avoid those situations and how to make it work. In order to do that, it is necessary to take very good notes about who is involved, what works, and what doesn't, all through the project. This is why it is *extremely* important that you, as a telecommuter, provide information about what works for you— and what doesn't—over the term of the project. In fact, one of the documents you are required to sign (Telecommuter's Agreement, included here) concentrates on that as one of the conditions for participating in the project.

Who are the telecommuters?

Participants in the project are being selected from many Company areas. They may include accountants, secretaries, managers, programmers, engineers, secretaries, administrative analysts, resource specialists, clerks—many sorts of "information workers." Basically, if your job primarily involves working with information, you are a potential telecommuter. However, because of some restrictions, such as the need to use very specialized (or very large) equipment, or the necessity to frequently interact with others face-to-face, not all information workers can be telecommuters—yet.

Do I HAVE to telecommute?

No. All of the participants in the project are volunteers. Furthermore, if, during the course of the project, you feel that you do not want to continue telecommuting then you are free to return to your job as it was before the project started. Likewise, if your immediate supervisor feels that telecommuting is not working out for you, you may also be asked to return to your former work pattern. It is also possible that changes in work circumstances, responsibilities, or assignment, may require that an employee be taken off the telecommuting project if doing so helps to better meet the immediate Company needs. Remember, the intent of the project is to evaluate telecommuting rather than to specially reward or penalize individual workers.

How many telecommuters are participating?

About 100.[3] Many of them will telecommute from home, the rest from telework centers at selected field locations as they become available. The telework center telecommuters will work at the center closest to their homes. Some telecommuters may do both: work from home some of the time, and from a telework center at other times. Not all telecommuters will begin at once. The formal implementation part of the project will run twelve months, beginning shortly after approval by the CEO. The first telecommuters will probably be home-based people, with telework-center-based telecommuting starting later.[4]

Who's in charge of the demonstration project?

Normal reporting relationships will not change. Your department has a project coordinator who will act in an advisory capacity to the Telecommuting Advisory Committee, which is responsible for advising the CEO on policy issues and reviewing progress of the demonstration project throughout its term. The overall project is being coordinated by the _____ Department. Your department coordinator should be contacted if you have questions about the operational details of the project.

Things You Should Know Before You Volunteer

There are a few other things that you should know before you volunteer to be a telecommuter or a telemanage. Here are some commonly asked questions ans answers about the details of the company telecommuting program.

Health and Safety for Home Telecommuters

What about accidents?

In order to maintain a businesslike atmosphere and minimize the chance of accidents, you are expected to keep your home office

---

[3] This is a critical question, to be answered during the planning phase of the project. A rule of thumb is that you should have enough participants to give statistical validity to any data you are taking during the evaluation phase. Don't forget that the standard error of a normal distribution is $1/N^{1/2}$, where N is the number of participants. That is, a survey involving 100 participants gives you a standard error of 10%; one with 1000 participants produces about a 3% error, etc. On the other hand, since telecommuting is still scary to a number of managers, you don't want to have so many initial telecommuters that management apprehension turns into panic.

[4] Or vice versa, depending on the extent of your facilities shortages/planning.

as clean and free from obstructions as if it were your regular Company office.

If you have a work-related accident at home you are expected to report it promptly. You are covered for such accidents as if they were in your principal office.

Will someone check out my home?
The Company reserves the right to do so, since it is ultimately responsible for ensuring that employees will have a safe work environment. Safety inspections may be made of the home office space prior to the beginning of the demonstration and at random times during the life of the demonstration. At least twenty-four hours prior notice will be given before any inspection. Basically, home-based telecommuters will be required to keep their office free of dangerous obstructions, loose wires, and other hazards. They should also have furniture, seating, acoustic isolation, and lighting that is conducive to a good work environment. Routine inspections during the project are not anticipated.

Equipment

Will I need a personal computer to telecommute?
Your job may not involve computer use and may still be perfectly "telecommutable." Telework center telecommuters may or may not need personal computers, depending on the details of their jobs. We expect that each telework center will have them.

Some home telecommuters may need only a telephone to work effectively. On the other hand, many home telecommuters will need either a personal computer or a data terminal and a modem for their work. If you regularly use a computer in your daily work, you may also need it at home. So all combinations of telephone or no-telephone, computer or no-computer are possible in the project.

Who's buying?
(Most government organizations we have surveyed do not provide additional equipment. Many large organizations that manufacture personal computers provide them for their telecommuters [usually older models]. Often, we find that telecommuters have better equipment at home than they do in their offices. Further, some departments in large organizations may decide to provide some equipment and/or software, while others don't.) Any such equipment or service provision is solely at the discretion of the Company. This will vary among the

participating departments or divisions. This equipment and software remains the property of the Company.

Who's responsible for maintenance?

The Company will be responsible for routine maintenance of Company-owned equipment and software used during the demonstration project. *However, it is each employee's responsibility to ensure that the equipment and software are used in businesslike conditions, whether at home or in a telework center.* This includes ensuring the equipment and software against abuse or other violation of existing policy of the Company concerning protection of its property.

Can I use the Company-provided equipment and/or software for personal purposes?

As long as your personal use of the equipment and/or software contributes to your proficiency with it, does not harm it, and does not conflict with other rules and regulations of the Company, you may use it for personal, non-business purposes.

Can I use my own equipment?

Yes, provided that it is compatible with the equipment used in the principal office. The responsibility for its maintenance and repair is still yours. Whether this occurs should be decided by your supervisor before you begin using the equipment.

Liability

What happens when something breaks or otherwise goes wrong?

You are responsible for immediately informing your supervisor. If you are conducting authorized Company business and your actions are within the course and scope of your employment, the Company's liability is the same whether you are at home, at a telework center or at your regular work location. This means that, unless your actions are fraudulent, corrupt, or there is actual malice, you will be indemnified by Company for any losses arising out of the use of your private property, both real and personal, for Company business.

If you interrupt Company business to do something that is not related to Company business and an accident occurs, then you are responsible just like any other homeowner.

Travel Expenses

Who pays for work-related travel?

Existing laws, and rules and contract provisions of the Company, are applicable to all the participants in the demonstration. On a case-by-case basis an employee's home, rather than the principal office may be designated as the headquarters for purposes of calculating mileage or per diem when the employee is required to make business trips.

If I'm a home telecommuter, do I get travel expenses for the times when I have to come in to the office for meetings?

No. Remember, a telecommuting day is one where the telecommuter works away from his or her regular workstation, either at a telework center or at home for the entire day. The telecommuting workstation becomes the "regular work station" for that day. Telecommuters and their supervisors would not normally schedule meetings, or travel, on days when the employee is scheduled for telecommuting.

Hours of Work

If I'm a home telecommuter, do I *have* to work at the telework office or at home all the time?

No. As a matter of fact, most telecommuters will spend several days per week at their principal office. Neither telework nor home telecommuting is an all-or-nothing situation; the idea is to work out a method for splitting your time between telework center or home and the principal office so that the tasks best done at the remote location (such as reading, letter and report writing, calculating, etc.) are done there, while the tasks best performed at the principal office (such as meetings) are done there. Note that *telecommuting is counted in whole days only*. That is, you have to average at least *one full day* per week[5] telecommuting over a six-month period to remain in the project. Two four-hour stints per week don't count.

Note that *average*, as used here means just that. We expect you to telecommute at least twenty-four full days[6] in a six-

---

[5] This requirement is in the rules because of air quality considerations. A significant part of commuting-related air pollution comes from cars being started. So the idea is to eliminate car starts altogether for home telecommuters. If a telecommuter comes in to the principal office for part of a day, the air quality advantage is mostly lost.

[6] The reason for this constraint is to ensure that each telecommuter has enough hours of telecommuting so that impacts measurements taken after a year's experience are with seasoned telecommuters. With only occasional telecommuters, many of the desired impacts on effectiveness, etc., may not have appeared.

month period. That does not mean that you have to telecommute one day each and every week. Some weeks you may need to telecommute several days, other weeks not at all. Telecommuting should be tailored to the demands of your job.

Do I *have* to work during the standard hours?
Your specific work periods must be arranged with your supervisor prior to your participation in the demonstration and may be revised at intervals throughout the project. Many telecommuters work when they feel most productive; often this is at times other than the standard office hours. Yet it may also be required that you can be contacted during specific work hours. Some telecommuters may be on a set schedule that coincides with their current work schedule.

What about sick leave and vacation?
You will accrue sick leave and vacation time at the same rate as you would in an ordinary office. If you are sick and unable to work in your home office, report those hours, as you would in a normal office setting. We anticipate that home telecommuters will use less sick leave than non-telecommuters; that has been the experience of other organizations involved in telecommuting. If you take abnormally high amounts of sick leave, or if you are not performing up to expectations in your home telecommuting, then we will ask that you discuss the problems with your supervisor if you haven't already done so. Your use of vacation, compensatory time off, sick leave, or any other type of leave is subject to approval by your supervisor, as usual.

What about overtime pay?
In all cases your regular hours of work, whether on a fixed or flexible schedule, must not exceed what is normal for you unless it is approved in advance by your supervisor. There will be no change in overtime. As before, prior approval of the supervisor is required for any overtime worked. Other types of premium pay, such as stand-by, lead, and shift pay, will not be affected by telecommuting.

Do I have to be glued in front of the computer all day?
Not at all. You might not even use a computer at all. Remember, the emphasis is on using these technologies to help you work better, not to dominate your life. If your job requires that you

spend time reading, meeting with others, talking on the phone, or just thinking, then that's what you should be doing.

Training

Is there any kind of telecommuter training?

Yes. Special workshops for telecommuters and their supervisors will be given before telecommuting begins. Each workshop will take about two hours. These workshops will emphasize the practical aspects of telecommuting: deciding when and how much to telecommute, setting up home offices (if applicable), scheduling meetings, keeping in touch with your fellow employees, and generally dealing with the problems and issues that may arise. Every telecommuter and his or her supervisor must enroll in one of these workshops prior to starting to telecommute.

There also will be a continuing series of meetings throughout the demonstration project during which fellow telecommuters can share experiences and ideas for improving telecommuting.

Performance and Workload Standards

Will performance standards change?

Performance standards and/or employee accountability for quantity and quality of output will not change during the demonstration project. What *may* change is your supervisor's method of monitoring and evaluating your performance in this new working relationship.

Who decides what my output should be?

You and your direct supervisor. The nature of telecommuting, the fact that you are out of sight for significant periods of time, requires that a high level of trust be built up between you and your supervisor. This means that you must accept more responsibility for getting the job done. It also means that you and your supervisor must discuss and ensure that you mutually understand what it is that you are expected to produce and when it is due.

What about work rules?

The standard work rules already established will still be officially in place during the demonstration project. However, we will be testing another set of performance and evaluation relationships at the same time. These relationships will be more oriented toward the results of your work than the ways in which you get it done. Therefore, if you and your supervisor feel that a nonstandard way of performing your job produces better results, then you may try it during the lifetime of the project. At the end of the project we will evaluate the results to see what works best for both the employees and the Company.

What about the security of the information I work with?

You are expected to follow all appropriate Company rules and regulations regarding security and confidentiality for your computer, its data and information, and any other information you handle. You are also expected to adhere to your department or division's policies and procedures.

Effects of Participation in the Project

How will participation in the demonstration project affect my promotability?

Telecommuting is just another way to do your job. Performance evaluations will be made as usual. The project is not designed or intended to affect your promotability.

Is it possible to leave the project after I've begun telecommuting?

You are always free to voluntarily return to your previous work mode if you feel pressured or if you feel that telecommuting is not right for you. However, we want to keep as many telecommuters as possible in the project throughout its lifetime. So please consider carefully your decision to participate.

Your supervisor may also terminate your participation in the project if your telecommuting, for any reason, is not working out.

It is also possible that changes in working circumstances, responsibilities, or assignment may require that an employee be taken off the telecommuting project in order to better meet the needs of the Company.

There will be no ill effects on your work record simply because of voluntary or involuntary termination of your participation in the project. On the other hand, you should realize that participation will not excuse you from operating within existing work rules and standards.

8

Measuring Results

— —·— —·— —— —·— —— —·— —·— —— —·— ——

In any organization that is based on economic survival for its continued existence—from families to multinational corporations, and even to governments—it is absolutely essential that the economic benefits of its efforts match or exceed the costs. This works for telecommuting as well. No organization will continue to use telecommuting if it decides that the costs do, or will eventually, outweigh the benefits.

Costs and benefits are not always measured in economic terms. Such hard-to-measure factors as quality-of-life and environmental impacts are also important for telecommuting.

The difficulty with telecommuting, as with most other aspects of information work, is that the typical accounting system usually measures the costs much more easily than the benefits. This chapter explores both costs and benefits, using my experience with real organizations as a basis for illustrating the issues. I have examined these experiences from four points of view:

- Amount and distribution of telecommuting
- Quality-of-life effects
- Work effectiveness changes
- Environmental impacts

Even though I am including some supposedly non-economic

factors in my results measurements, I have tried to relate them to economic measures.

Data Source

The rest of the material in this chapter is based on the final results of a multi-year telecommuting demonstration project in a large urban-based organization with more than 45,000 employees, about 40% of whom are information workers. The organization tested telecommuting primarily in response to the demands of air quality regulations. The data reported here were derived from a number of sources: questionnaires given at roughly 9-month intervals to more than 300 telecommuters, their non-telecommuting co-workers, and their supervisors; departmental cost records; and direct interviews of the participants. The participants in the project came from more than 20 different departments and included a wide spectrum of job types, most of them mid-level. The organization also followed the guidelines in this book. Although the numbers given here are from this one organization, the results are similar to those I have obtained from a number of different organizations and can be considered fairly typical.

Beginning Telecommuting

My experience has been that both the costs and the benefits of telecommuting change with time. The costs tend to be up-front, even before telecommuting begins. The benefits per telecommuter tend to increase with time, growing even after two years of telecommuting. In a typical program, telecommuting begins with a relatively small proportion of the organization's workforce,[1] so that the initial impacts are equally small. Also typically, the initial complement of telecommuters tend to be among the upper half of the employees in terms of proven performance.

Therefore, the absolute results (that is, annual net dollars) after the first year or two may be higher per telecommuter than in later years when less-capable telecommuters have joined the group. However, the proportional results tend to match the early

---

[1] In a large organization, say one with tens of thousands of employees, only a few hundred telecommuters—1% or 2% of the information workers—may be involved in the initial project

results as the programs expand. That is, while the first group may represent only a few percent of the information workers, they may represent a much larger percent of the organization's productivity base. As workers of lower base productivity are added, their per capita marginal dollar contribution to overall organizational productivity is lower.

Table 8-1: ACTIVITIES PERFORMED WHILE TELECOMMUTING

Activity	% who engaged in it
Thinking or planning	69.2
Reading	68.6
Text or word processing	58.3
Writing (without a computer)	55.1
Research	55.1
Coordinating by telephone	44.9
Working with data bases	22.4
Computer programming	20.5
Other	20.5
Record keeping	17.3
Graphics or layout	10.9
Coordinating via computer	8.3
Having meetings	2.0

The nominal initial goal for the project described here was to have participants telecommuting at least one day per week, on average. Some jobs are suitable for practically full-time telecommuting, in my experience, while others might encounter difficulty reaching the one-day-per-week goal, given early 1990s technology availability. Some of the telecommuters found that they could not continue telecommuting at the same rate that they tried the first month. Others found that they could increase their rate of telecommuting. Still others maintained their original rate. The overall average for the first month of telecommuting was 4.0 days, with median and mode also at 4 days and the range going from 1 to 23 days. For the first month of their telecommuting, 99% of the telecommuters worked at home 8 days or less.

In practice, the number of telecommuting days per month tends to increase over time. An analysis of the historic data for this particular project shows an expected average of 4.2 days per month for those who have been telecommuting for a year. Telecommuters with 2 years of experience are likely to be telecommuting about 8 days per month. For comparison, another project, involving telecommuters from a broader geographical area, showed an average of 5.2 days per month at the end of the first year of telecommuting and 6.5 days per month at the end of the second year. A linear regression analysis[2] of the telecommuting frequency data indicates that the telecommuters will tend to telecommute about 2.4 days per week as they gain experience with telecommuting. Figure 8-1 shows the regression line, slightly modified for the first 10 months.

Figure 8-1 *Projected Telecommuting Rates*

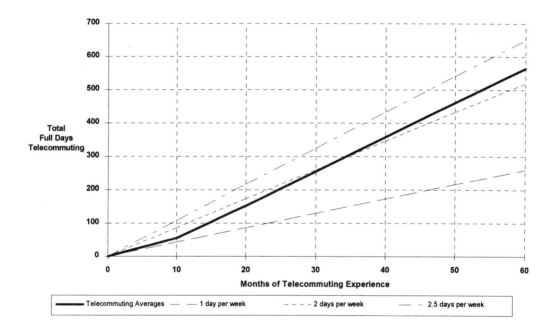

One concern with telecommuting is whether it will increase car use, since an "extra" car may be available when the telecommuter is working at home. Twenty-three percent of the telecommuters said that the car was indeed used by themselves or someone else in their household when they worked at home (the

---

[2] Linear regression is a statistical procedure that fits a straight line to a set of data points. In this case the data points are length of time telecommuting and the number of telecommuting days during that period.

remaining 77% maintained that it was not in use). *Of those who stated that their car was available, 23% (6% of all the telecommuters) stated that there was an overall decrease in non-commuting car use in addition to the decrease due to telecommuting!* To counter this, another 23% (6% of all the telecommuters) stated that there was some additional car use, but not enough to counteract the telecommuting reduction. An additional 5% of the car-available group (1% of all telecommuters) said that their added non-commuting car use acted to cancel the reduction from telecommuting. In summary, only 8% of the telecommuters reported any erosion of the car use savings.

Analysis of detailed trip logs that were administered to the telecommuter households, showed that some of this additional car use was the result of telecommuters performing chores that otherwise would have been carried out by other family members. Hence, the slight additional use of their cars by some telecommuters may be overstated, since many of the "new" trips replace trips that would have occurred anyway. The net result of the actual trip measurements was an overall reduction in car use over and above the telecommuting reduction. To be conservative, I concluded that telecommuting produced exactly the car use reduction that equaled the reduction in commute trips. Therefore, it completely satisfied the primary goal of the project: telecommuting-eliminated trips are not replaced by other trips.

The average telecommuter allocated about 37% of his or her weekly work tasks for the telecommuting period. Given the overall average of 0.9 days per week telecommuting for this group, that works out to *37% of the work being accomplished in 18% to 23% of the work week; possibly an average 100% productivity increase per telecommuting day.* Table 0 shows what the telecommuters were doing when they telecommuted. While 17.5% of the telecommuters viewed telecommuting as a temporary or occasional thing, 82.5% considered it to be a permanent change to their working ways.

Quality-of-Life Effects

Aside from the quantitative effects of telecommuting, there is the issue of the socio-psychological effects of telecommuting. What is the impact of telecommuting on the telecommuters and their families? We did not develop direct evidence of the effects on the families during these projects; rather we asked the telecommuters about the impacts. We included a section in our evaluation questionnaires specifically oriented toward these impacts. Common factor analysis[3] of the questionnaires allowed us to break a number of the work or social impacts into eleven categories, as follows:

- *General Work Life.* This relates to changes in the individual's relationships with his or her supervisor, self-assessment of job skills, feelings of job responsibility, influence, versatility, and scope.
- *Personal Life.* This factor includes changes in quality of family relationships, discretionary time, feelings of control of one's life, ability to separate work and home life, success in self-discipline, coordination of family and work time, and knowing when to quit work.

Table 8-2: WORK OR SOCIAL FACTOR CHANGES

Factor	Telecommuters	Non-Telecommuters	Difference (T - non-T)
Liberation	4.9	1.6	3.2
Continuity	3.1	1.3	1.7
Creativity	3.2	1.3	1.9
Personal Life	2.5	1.0	1.5
Environmental Influences	2.2	0.6	1.6
General Work Life	2.2	1.0	1.1
Stress Avoidance	1.2	0.3	0.9
Interdependence	1.0	0.5	0.5
Visibility	0.9	0.4	0.5
Belonging	0.6	0.3	0.3
Apprehension	0.7	0.6	0.1

- *Visibility.* Do telecommuters feel out of their supervisor's and co-workers' minds when they're out of sight? This factor includes changes in one's influence on organizational strategy,

---

[3] Factor analysis is a statistical technique that helps analyze questionnaire items in terms of groups of closely related questions. That is, if question X in a group was answered with a certain value, the likelihood is high that another question in the same group would be answered the same way. In this case, the participants were given a set of 50 questions that related to quality-of-life impacts; the analysis showed that the responses could be associated into 11 groups.

understanding of what others are doing, how well one's suggestions are received, and self-assessment of visibility in the organization.

- *Environmental Influences.* This includes changes in home office space, stress from environmental noise, ability to match work and biorhythms, and feelings of self-empowerment.

Figure 8-2 *A "Radar" View of the Quality-of-life Changes*

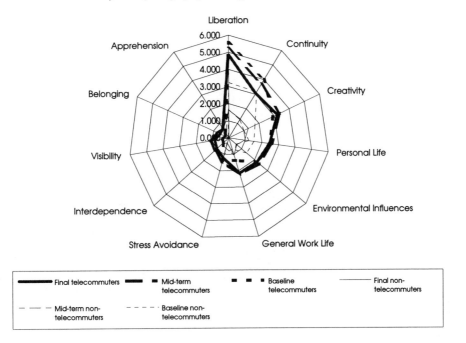

- *Belonging.* Do telecommuters feel themselves to be loners? Here we have changes in involvement in office social activities, amount of job-related feedback, career advancement, job stability, and relationships with fellow workers.
- *Creativity.* Changes in: creativity in one's work, the amount of flexibility in job performance and feelings of self-empowerment, are in this factor.
- *Stress Avoidance.* Changes in work-related costs, ability to bypass physical handicaps, and avoidance of office politics are grouped here.
- *Liberation.* This factor includes changes in ability to concentrate on crucial tasks, the need to cope with traffic, and the ability to get more done.

- *Apprehension.* Changes in uneasiness about equipment failure and feelings of guilt about "not really working" constitute this category.
- *Interdependence.* This factor relates to changes in the quality of meetings with colleagues and dependence on others to help perform one's job.
- *Continuity.* The final factor calibrates changes in freedom from interruptions.

Figure 8-3 *Comparative Quality-of-life Changes*

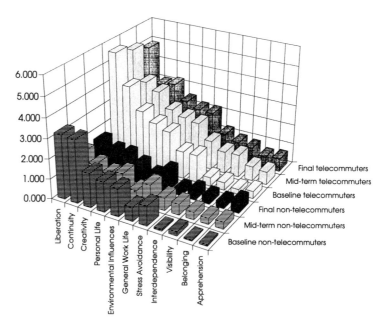

Note that the emphasis is on *changes* in these categories. We asked the participants what had changed since telecommuting began, whether or not they were telecommuters. We asked how much, if any, change there was and how important each issue was to them. We developed composite values (amount of change multiplied by importance to the participant) for these factors, as shown in Table 8-2. The scales for amount of change are from -2 to +2, with -2 signifying much worse, 0 meaning no change, and +2 signifying much better. Importance ranges from 0 (not important at all) to 4 (extremely important to the participant).

Thus, the composite factor can range from -8 (i.e., -2 × 4) to +8 (i.e., +2 × 4).

The surveys showed clear differences between the telecommuter and non-telecommuter groups. There are three areas in which we might expect to see negative impacts from telecommuting: Visibility, Apprehension and Belonging. Yet, this group of telecommuters, on average, showed net positive changes for all three, although there were some individual negative responses.

Figures 8-2 and 8-3 show two different views of the elements of Table 8-2 as well as the comparable results from the mid-term (first nine months) and baseline (start-of-telecommuting) surveys. Note that, with the exception of the liberation and continuity factors, both groups at mid-term appear to be more positive than they were during the baseline survey; then both groups tended to decline slightly from the mid-term to final surveys. In two of the key factors—continuity and creativity— the telecommuter group switched rankings between the mid-term and final surveys, while the non-telecommuters stayed about the same. This could arise from a possible increase in interruptions to the telecommuters as more people got used to contacting them while they were at home, coupled with a decrease in interruptions in the office as the on-site office population decreased. Interestingly, the telecommuters' responses to the liberation and continuity factors declined after the baseline measure, showing the effects of reality slightly modifying expectations.

In any case, the telecommuters showed quality-of-life changes that were more positive in every respect than those of the non-telecommuters.

Effectiveness Changes

An important criterion in assessing the desirability of telecommuting is its impact on employee effectiveness. As a minimum acceptance criterion, overall work performance should not degrade from its pre-telecommuting values. As was the case with the quality-of-life factors, I concentrated on assessing changes in, rather than absolute values of, worker effectiveness. Several indirect measures of effectiveness factors were included in our evaluating survey questionnaires. However, the most numerically clear test is a direct question asking each respondent—and her or his direct supervisor—whether, and how much, their effectiveness changed since telecommuting began.

Quantitative Estimates

Of the group of telecommuters, the range in their self-estimate responses ran from no change to increases of 100%. The average response for all the reporting telecommuters was an increase of 30% with a median response of a 25% increase. In the case of the non-telecommuters, the range in responses ran from a decrease of 50% to an increase of 100%.[4] The average response for the non-telecommuters was an increase of 24%, with a median response of 20%. The difference between the telecommuters' and non-telecommuters' average self-estimates of effectiveness change was 6%. The difference was significant at the 0.09 level.[5] About 13% of the telecommuters and 25% of the non-telecommuters indicated no change in their effectiveness since telecommuting began.

Table 8-3: ESTIMATES OF EFFECTIVENESS INCREASES BY LEVEL OF TRAINING

Training Received by:	Supervisors' Estimates		Self-Estimates	
	Telecommuters	Non-Tele-commuters	Telecommuters	Non-Tele-commuters
Neither	21.4%	6.0%	33.3%	21.3%
Telecommuter only	14.7%	11.0%	31.8%	21.2%
Supervisor only	38.3%	8.8%	30.7%	33.0%
Both	23.3%	12.5%	28.9%	26.9%

Note that the above figures are derived from the *employees'* responses. Typically, supervisors' estimates of employee effectiveness are lower than those of the employees themselves. We also surveyed the participants' supervisors. The supervisors' estimates of the telecommuters' effectiveness changes averaged 22%; their estimate of non-telecommuters' effectiveness changes averaged 9%, a difference of 14%. In this case, the difference was

---

[4] Non-telecommuters can increase their effectiveness through such means as more experience or training, fewer interruptions from (telecommuting or other) co-workers, greater maturity in work attitudes, etc.

[5] That is, the odds are 10 to 1 in favor of the difference being meaningful.

significant at the .008 level.[6] Twenty-five percent of the telecommuters' supervisors and 48% of the non-telecommuters' supervisors indicated no change in effectiveness. Hence, the telecommuters showed clear effectiveness improvements relative to the non-telecommuters, particularly in the estimation of their supervisors.

There were some clear differences of opinion between supervisor and employee concerning effectiveness change. The telecommuters' self-estimates tended to agree more closely with that of their supervisors. Nineteen percent of the telecommuters and supervisors agreed exactly on the effectiveness changes; only 8% of the supervisors and non-telecommuters agreed. Twenty-six percent of the telecommuters received higher ratings from their supervisors than they gave themselves. Twenty-one percent of the non-telecommuters received higher than their self-ratings from their supervisors. The most interesting aspect of these results is that the supervisors' estimates differ much more between telecommuters and non-telecommuters than do the individuals' self-estimates.

Training Influences

One of the elements of the analysis is to see whether the initial training sessions for the project had any influence on the effectiveness outcomes. Table 8-3 shows the effectiveness estimates as a function of who was trained. A direct reading of the table can be slightly misleading, since there are only a few cases among the telecommuters where either no one or only the supervisor was trained. The overall evidence is that it is particularly important that supervisors receive training.

Environmental Impacts

The most important environmental impacts of telecommuting come from the fact that most home-based telecommuters do not drive during their telecommuting days. These telecommuters are reducing their daily air pollution production and energy use. At the individual level this may not seem like much but, magnified by thousands or millions of telecommuters, it can become a major means of improving environmental quality.

---

[6] Here, the odds are 127 to 1 in favor of a meaningful difference.

Air Pollution

For our example case of an organization with about 16,000 telecommuters working from home an average of 1.4 days per week, the annual pollution reduction would be on the order of:

- 6,150,000 pounds of carbon monoxide;
- 380,000 pounds of nitrogen oxides;
- 1,150,000 pounds of unburned hydrocarbons; and
- 26,000 pounds of particulates.

As a further example, Figure 8-4 shows the annual levels of reduced car mileage for the Los Angeles CMSA[7] under what appears to be the current telecommuting growth trend in the area.

Figure 8-4   *Annual Mileage Reductions from Telecommuting: High Growth Scenario*

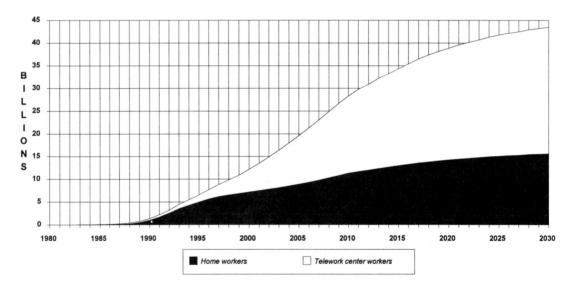

Since at least half of this mileage reduction involves automobile cold starts—the most polluting phase of car use—telecommuting promises to be a significant reducer of air pollution in coming years. Figure 8-5 shows the area-wide pollution reduction impacts for that trend. Since the pollution reduction data were calculated using a constant ratio of pollutants per vehicle-mile, the results are somewhat understated for the 1990s and, perhaps, overstated for the years past 2000.

---

[7] Combined Metropolitan Statistical Area, an area in southern California that includes almost half of California's population.

The early understatement is because the data used were for highway travel in the mid-1980s and did not include an increase in pollution for the startup and idling periods. An overstatement could result from a steady improvement, over the mid-1980s levels, in the quantity of pollutants emitted by cars.

For comparison, air pollution data from California's South Coast Air Quality Management District show the annual pollution contribution from cars in 1991 to be 1,580,000 tons of carbon monoxide, 221,000 tons of hydrocarbons, 243,000 tons of nitrogen oxides, and 20,000 tons of particulates. If the telecommuting growth trend of Figure 8-5 continues, we could expect reductions by the year 2000 of 19%, 23%, 8%, and 4%, respectively, from present levels.

Figure 8-5 *Air Pollution Reductions from Telecommuting: High Growth Scenario*

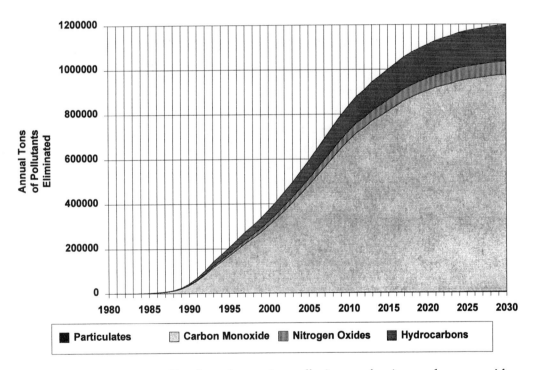

Clearly, these air pollution reduction values provide a persuasive argument for further development of telecommuting. In addition to the air pollution factors, there are the energy conservation consequences of telecommuting. My forecast model calculates the net effect of telecommuting on energy conservation. The net effect is derived from the reduction in automobile fuel use by telecommuters, combined with the possibly increased use of computers and the clearly increased use of telecommunications.

Energy Consumption

My forecast of the energy conservation impacts of telecommuting is based on my analysis of the commuting patterns of thousands of urban area employees. The particular estimate shown here is derived from a 1990 survey of the employees of our example organization. The average estimated one-way commute distance for these employees was 19.8 miles, slightly less than that of the telecommuters in the project.

I also assumed that future telecommuters would have the same pattern of compressed work week schedules (that is, fewer work days per week but more hours per work day) as were followed by the employees in 1991. This produces an average effective work week of 4.8 days. The telecommuting rate was assumed to be an average of 1.4 days per week—all from home—based on the observed trends among the telecommuters.

The calculations produced an average annual energy saving of 4,200 kilowatt-hours per telecommuter,[8] for a total annual saving, assuming about 16,000 active telecommuters, of 60 million kilowatt-hours, about 1,600,000 gallons of gasoline.

The forecast model calculates the net effect of telecommuting on energy conservation. The net effect is derived from the reduction in automobile fuel use by telecommuters, partially offset by the possibly increased use of computers and the clearly increased use of telecommunications.

Three factors are not included in the model. First, notwithstanding the contrary experience of our sample project, I expect that telecommuters will tend to use slightly more home heating and cooling energy while they are telecommuting. At present, there are no data to show an offset of this energy use by a comparable reduction in the heating and cooling of the "downtown" offices of the telecommuters—largely because there are not yet enough telecommuters for the effects to be noticeable. The model assumes a wash between these two energy uses in the long run.

---

[8] This is a conservative estimate, based on a lower rate of telecommuting than I think will actually occur in a few years. The cost-benefit model later in this chapter uses a higher figure: 6,000 kilowatt-hours per annum.

Second, the model does not include my finding that about 20% of telecommuter households have a reduction in car use over and above the telecommuting-specific reduction.[9] Given these caveats, I feel that the projections shown in Figure 8-6 provide a conservative estimate of home-based telecommuting's energy impacts.

Third, the model assumes only home-based telecommuting. Telecommuting from telework centers is more problematic in its environmental impacts. The key is whether or not telework center telecommuters drive to work. If they walk or bike to work, ride share (without driving to the ride share pick up point), or take some form of mass transit, then the impacts are as shown for the home-based telecommuters. If they drive to the telework center, then the environmental improvements may be substantially reduced.

Figure 8-6 *Estimated Area-Wide Energy Conservation Impacts of Telecommuting.*

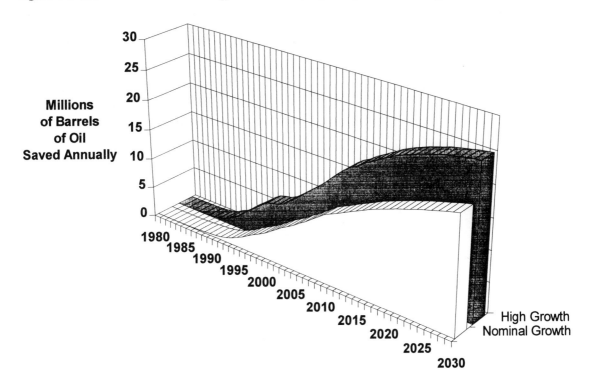

---

[9] See our report: *Telecommuting Travel Impact Analysis: Los Angeles Telecommuting Pilot Project* for details.

In reality, there will be a mixed bag of environmental results for a few years. Most contemporary telecommuters are home-based. Most telework centers at first were regional centers that reduced, but did not eliminate, driving to work by telecommuters. Therefore, the environmental improvement produced by these centers is only partial. Beginning in late 1993, California began testing the feasibility of neighborhood telework centers. These centers, as defined in Chapter 1, are located to service neighborhood residents who walk or bike to work. For them the environmental impacts are essentially the same as for home-based telecommuting.

Cost and Benefit Considerations

A key issue in evaluating telecommuting, or any other change in organizational behavior, is whether the net economic result—the infamous bottom line—is positive, neutral or negative. Although some factors, such as quality of work life, necessarily must be somewhat subjective, other factors can be quantified relatively readily. I have also included actual measured costs and benefits to date. The costs include the time-plus-overhead costs of the employees who participated in project administration. The numbers in the cost-benefit model reported here are for 300 active telecommuters in our sample organization.

Costs

These are the main factors for analysis.

Direct Costs

There are twelve main cost categories:

- Additional training
- Telecommunications hardware, software and operating costs
- Computer hardware and software
- Moving expenses
- Facilities leasing
- Construction costs
- Furniture
- Insurance
- Miscellaneous rental
- Project administration

- Additional travel
- Liability

In most cases the costs are quantifiable relatively easily and are available routinely. In some cases the costs must be estimated. This approach of including quantifiable as well as estimated costs provides a conservative view of a project, so that the actual costs might be lower than those shown here.

Additional Training. This category deals with the costs for training that are specifically telecommuting-related (for example, interpersonal communications and management instruction). Training costs may be computed as the total of time spent by the trainer and trainees, times their respective hourly rates (including indirect costs), plus costs of equipment and materials used for training. Training costs for the more than 400 employees (and their supervisors, etc.) who were trained in the example project were estimated at about $65,000, or $150 per trained telecommuter. This figure includes the costs of the organization's personnel who were involved in administering or coordinating the training sessions, amounting to 34% of the total. Per capita training costs may decrease with time, both as the training becomes more efficient and as telecommuting becomes an integral part of the organization's normal culture.

Telecommunications. Telecommunications costs (such as equipment purchase or lease, software services, etc.) can be primarily telecommuting-related or, as in the case of training costs, may be incurred as a normal part of office automation with telecommuting accounting only for some of the additional service charges. This allocation must also be made on a case-by-case basis. This particular employer did not provide any telecommunications equipment for the telecommuters. The final survey shows that the telecommuters had an average monthly telephone bill of $3.59 more than the non-telecommuters, but a median telephone cost of $7.50 *less* than the non-telecommuters. I could not determine the costs of additional calls from the office to telecommuters' homes, as the organization's telephone billing system does not break out such calls. I have found that this situation is fairly common.

For the sake of conservatism in the benefit-cost model, I assumed that the average telecommuter telephone bill increased $4 per month ($48 per year) and that there was a corresponding

$48 annual increase in office-to-home telephone charges for telecommuters.

Computers. Computer charges could constitute the largest portion of a telecommuting budget, depending on how they are allocated. These are the options:

- *Total Duplication*. These are cases where a computer is purchased solely because of telecommuting. Either there would be no computer use by an employee except for telecommuting, or there would be no duplication of computers without telecommuting. For these cases, all the computer costs should be charged to telecommuting.
- *Partial Duplication*. If the computer capabilities would be made available to an employee in any case, then only those costs peculiar to the telecommuting situation (such as telecommunications interconnect equipment purchase or lease, make-ready costs, software, maintenance, etc.) should be charged to telecommuting.
- *No Duplication*. This covers cases where either the telecommuter does not use a computer while telecommuting, or where the necessary equipment and software is already owned by the telecommuter (telecommuters' costs are analyzed separately), or where necessary software duplication is allowed without charge by the software providers and no computer communications software or hardware is used.

At present, I know of no cases of total duplication by the employer among the organizations with which I have dealt, and only a few cases of partial duplication, generally involving duplicate software packages for telecommuters' own personal computers at home. In general, almost no computer charges were incurred by the organization represented here. However, in many cases this is because employees who were trained and needed computers were not allowed to telecommute because they did not have computers at home and employer-supplied computers were not available. Over 70% of the active telecommuters in this organization owned their own computers and used them for telecommuting by the end of the project. Those employees invested just over $100,000 in telecommuting-specific computer hardware, software, furniture, office equipment, telephone services and maintenance during the last year of the project.[10] More than half, 56%, made no telecommuting-specific investments in equipment. Note that, of those who did invest in equipment, about 85% of their total investment was specifically related to telecommuting. For conservatism, I estimated that the investment required for the average new computer-using telecommuter will be about $2,000, to be made either by the telecommuter or by the employer. For the purposes of the benefit-cost model, I assumed that the employer will make this purchase for 40% of the telecommuters added each year after the end of the demonstration project.

Moving Costs. This category includes all the costs of moving existing equipment from offices to either homes or satellite center offices. It also includes telephone installation costs and costs of any related interoffice moves by non-telecommuters. There were no costs for moving telecommuters on the part of our example employer. I was not able to assess costs of moving non-telecommuters. Therefore, this amount is zero in my current model.

Facilities Leasing. This cost applies to any telework center set up as part of the telecommuting program. The differential cost should be charged here. That is, the cost of the leased space (or amortized purchase or construction costs) minus the cost of any space eliminated from the inventory of the facility previously occupied by the telecommuter(s). Our example organization had no telework centers; all telecommuters were home-based. Therefore, this amount is zero in the benefit-cost model.

Administration. There are several components of the administrative costs of telecommuting, some of which are difficult to assess. These include the special management costs of the pilot project itself (including evaluation); telecommuting-related changes in the administrative system of the employer (such as changes in time accounting); possible duplication of effort or supplies caused by telecommuting; and costs of system integration and coordination. Administrative costs include part of the salaries of the Project Manager, the department coordinators and consulting costs other than training. I estimated the total administrative costs for the completed demonstration

---

[10] The per-telecommuter cost for those who made telecommuting-specific investments averaged $2000, split into $1840 for hardware and $210 for software that was telecommuting-specific.

project at $307,000, including the planning phase of the project—about $700 per trained telecommuter.

Additional Travel. This category applies to two factors:

- Managers and professionals who find themselves traveling between their "home" offices and other centers during the day for meetings that would otherwise require only a short walk to a conference room
- Losses to car- and van-pools because of telecommuters who no longer use them

None of these costs appeared in the example project. Although some telecommuters were members of car- or van-pools, their participation as telecommuters did not appear to have disturbed the pools significantly, according to our interviews and trip survey data.

Liability Costs. One largely unresolved factor is the possibility of increased exposure to worker's compensation claims resulting from work-related accidents in the homes of telecommuters. Although I do not know of any worker's compensation claims arising to date from telecommuting in any organization, this factor is included for informational purposes. No participants in the example project have claimed telecommuting-related worker's compensation claims.

Indirect Costs

The following are indirect cost factors that are analyzed, since they relate to general support of office work.

Increased Building Energy Consumption. Shifting work to homes, or to smaller buildings characteristic of telework centers, may increase or decrease energy consumption related to space heating and cooling. Persuasive arguments have been made to support either net increases or net decreases in building energy use.

To estimate this I checked the differences in between average reported home gas and electric bills. Telecommuters paid an average of $4.01 *more* for electricity and $4.51 *less* for gas than the members of the control group, for a net energy cost decrease of $0.50 per month per telecommuter. For conservatism I assumed that there was no change in the energy consumption of employer office facilities when the telecommuters were away from those offices. My conclusion is that there was no significant difference between telecommuters and non-telecommuters in building energy consumption.[11]

Increased Local Traffic Congestion. By diverting automobile traffic from freeways to local streets, telework center telecommuting may cause an increase in local traffic congestion, with associated energy and pollution costs. On the other hand, one objective of local and neighborhood telework centers was to reduce the fraction of telecommuters who still drive (rather than walk or bicycle) to work. I have no clear data of any effect one way or the other. Therefore, it is set as zero in the model.

Benefits

Direct Benefits

Although many of the cost elements are easily established, many of the benefits of telecommuting are less easily defined in quantitative terms. Most important of these benefits is employee effectiveness. The following are the benefit factors that generally appear in non-quantitative terms.

Increased Employee Effectiveness including output quality and quantity. I compute the effectiveness impact by multiplying the estimated effectiveness change by the individual's salary. If we adopt the conservative view that the differential effectiveness change of the telecommuters (that is, the telecommuter estimates minus the non-telecommuter estimates) is that of the employees, then the monthly effectiveness-change-benefit per telecommuter after 18 months or so of telecommuting is about $369 (as contrasted with $344 at the project midpoint and $155 after a few weeks of telecommuting). If we average the supervisor's and employee's estimates we get a monthly effectiveness-change-benefit of $642 (as compared to $508 at the mid-term evaluation and $295 in the baseline survey). If all of the employer's 400-odd telecommuters maintained or increased

---

[11] As a counter example, the author's tele-office has two high-end personal computers and monitors running 24 hours per day, every day including weekends, plus a laser printer and other computer accessories, lighting, etc.. The office is electrically air conditioned. The total annual energy use of the office is about 1900 kWh. The annual cost of this (all in electricity use) is $176, or about $14.70 per month (about the cost of ten gallons of gasoline). Ten gallons of gasoline will suffice for about six round trips between the author's office and downtown Los Angeles.

these effectiveness differences in the future, then the annual benefit would be between $1,920,000 and $3,330,800, depending on one's point of view.

The average telecommuters' self-estimate of effectiveness change increased by 19% between the final and mid-term surveys, and by 22% between the baseline and midterm surveys, while the non-telecommuters' self estimates increased by 41% between the final and mid-term surveys, and decreased by 7%. between the mid-term and baseline surveys. The supervisors' estimates of their telecommuters' effectiveness changes increased by about 28% between the final and mid-term surveys, while their estimates of non-telecommuters' effectiveness decreased by about 2%. The mid-term estimates from the supervisors showed about the same amount (46% and 50%, respectively) for both groups over the baseline estimates. The conclusion is that the telecommuters' effectiveness was still increasing at the end of the project, while the non-telecommuters' effectiveness was staying about the same, at least in the estimates of their supervisors.

- *Decreased Sick Leave* can be derived from employee records. My conclusion from the data derived to date is that telecommuters will take two days less sick leave per year.

- *Decreased Medical Costs* are difficult to assess. No one has performed a long-term study of the health impacts of telecommuting. For the time being, I assume this impact is zero. However, I expect long term medical costs to decrease for telecommuters because of the clear reductions in stress stated by participants in our focus group sessions. These benefits are not likely to show up in statistically significant terms for several years.

- *Increased Organization Effectiveness* including output quality and quantity. A quantitative answer to this question requires a survey that has not yet been made, to the best of my knowledge. Anecdotal evidence from focus group meetings leads us to believe that there is a slight overall increase in effectiveness of the telecommuters' organizations. That is, effectiveness is also increasing among the non-telecommuting office mates of the telecommuters. This is primarily because the non-telecommuters also became better organized because of telecommuting. For the purposes of the benefit-cost model, I estimate that the improvement, in dollar terms, amounts to 0.5% of the telecommuters' salaries (that is, about 3% of the supervisor-estimated effectiveness increase of the non-telecommuters).

- *Decreased Turnover* and attendant reductions in personnel search, hiring, and training costs. Of the telecommuter respondents, 23% replied that they had seriously considered quitting. Among that number, 74% (or 18% of all the telecommuters) said the ability to telecommute was a moderate to decisive influence on their decision to stay. My conservative estimate is that it would cost about 25% of the departing telecommuters' annual salaries if they had to be completely replaced.[12] I multiply this by an additional factor (ranging from 0 to 1) related to the influence of telecommuting on their decision to stay. The computed result was a benefit of about $206,000 for the group of about 160 telecommuters who completed this portion of the final questionnaire.
- *Reduced Parking Requirements.* If advantage were taken of the fact that telecommuters are not using parking space part of the time, and the space were reassigned to, or used by, non-telecommuters, then the monthly savings would be roughly one-fourth of the $90 monthly parking cost per telecommuter, or about $22.
- *Office Space Saving* as telecommuters share office space. We did not yet test office space saving methods for this particular employer. However, my experience with other organizations indicates that companies or government agencies with large numbers of home-based telecommuters can readily achieve up to 33% reductions in office space. In the case of some departments of our example employer, telecommuting allowed existing groups to work more effectively with what was previously severe overcrowding. To be conservative, I set this factor at zero for the cost-benefit model.
- *Increased Ability to Attract Staff* as prospective employees consider telecommuting an attractive work option. Although this is related to the turnover reduction benefit, I was not able to get unambiguous data on the impacts. This factor has been used successfully by other organizations, particularly

---

[12] For highly skilled individuals the figure can be significantly higher. For example, G. Alan Hunter of the California Franchise Tax Board estimated that the cost of replacing a skilled auditor of multinational corporations is more than $100,000.

government agencies, as a hiring tool. I did not count it as a benefit in the model.

Indirect Benefits

As with the cost elements, there are indirect benefits, some of which are most easily measured in dollar terms. These are largely related to reduced use of automobile transportation, as the following will indicate.

- *Decreased Energy Consumption* as commuter automobiles are not used. I estimate that the average telecommuters' energy use reduction, assuming current telecommuting trends persist,[13] will run in excess of 6,000 kilowatt-hours per year.

Figure 8-7 *Summary of Project Costs and Benefits*

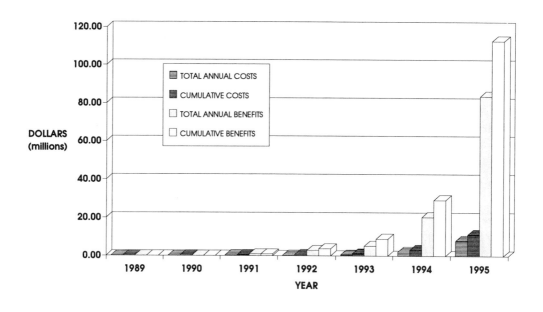

<hr />

[13] That is, a continuing trend toward telecommuting an average of two days per week, replacing an average round trip of 45.7 miles, with 10% rideshare offset and an average car fuel efficiency of 24 miles per gallon. The average work week is 4.7 days for this group of telecommuters, since many are also on modified work schedules, with an average of 49 weeks worked per year. This produces a total annual saving of 187 gallons of gasoline (or about 6800

At a gasoline price of $1.30 per gallon, this amounts to an annual saving of about $214 per telecommuter. Although there is no direct saving to the employer, there may be an implicit saving in decreased wage demands by telecommuters.

- *Decreased Air Pollution.* The air pollution reduction is directly proportional to the overall decrease in automobile use. However, dollar costs of air pollution are difficult to establish, are not generally assessed directly to the employer, and are not included here.

Figure 8-8 *Summary of Benefit-to-Cost Ratios*

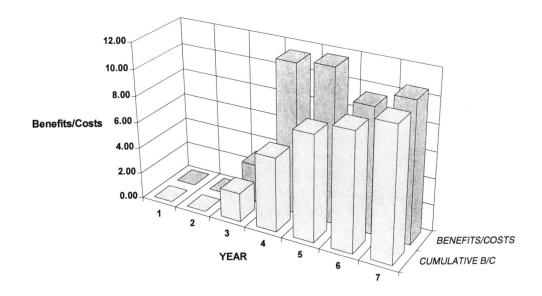

- *Decreased Traffic Congestion.* As in the air pollution case, it is difficult to make a firm estimate of the dollar costs of traffic congestion. An indirect measure is that of a primary impetus for the telecommuting project: If the Southern California employer that is our example does not increase its average vehicle ridership to satisfactory levels, it may be liable for fines of $25,000 per day of non-compliance with Regulation XV of the South Coast Air Quality Management District.

kilowatt-hours) per telecommuter. We deduct 800 kilowatt-hours to account for any additional home energy use.

This pollution penalty trend, although apparently originated in Southern California, is migrating to the rest of the world as urban air pollution problems worsen.

- *Increased Access for the Mobility Handicapped* including disabled, working parents, retirees, etc. The group of telecommuters includes individuals with mobility handicaps. Their reactions in this respect are included in the overall improvements in quality-of-life indicated by the telecommuters. However, indirect benefits in this category include the reductions in welfare costs as a result of returning people to the active workforce via telecommuting.

Results

Employer

The factors above have been included in a cost-benefit model. The major one-time project costs are those of the project itself: planning, selection, training, evaluation, and administration. These costs cease at the end of the project. Recurring costs are primarily those of telecommunications (phone charges) and training. All of the benefits are recurring. Figure 8-7 shows the historical and expected costs and benefits from the development of the project plan through completion of the evaluation phase and three years thereafter. The figure includes an assumption that telecommuting will increase after completion of the demonstration project. The assumed growth shown here was to 600 telecommuters in the first year, 2,400 in the second year, and 9,600 in the third year after the end of the demonstration

Table 8-4: SUMMARY OF THE BENEFIT-COST MODEL (COSTS IN $ MILLIONS)

YEAR	1	2	3	4	5	6	7
No. of telecommuters	0	0	211	300	600	2400	9600
Total annual costs	0.05	0.06	0.30	0.25	0.44	2.39	9.57
Total annual benefits	0.00	0.00	0.90	2.82	5.19	21.65	90.37
Cumulative costs	0.05	0.11	0.41	0.66	1.10	3.50	13.06
Cumulative benefits	0.00	0.00	0.90	3.72	8.91	30.56	120.93
Benefits/Costs	0.00	0.00	2.96	11.36	11.68	9.05	9.45
Cumulative B/C	0.00	0.00	2.18	5.63	8.06	8.74	9.26
Development costs	0.048	0.041	0.086	0.157	0.034	0.810	3.240
Operating costs	0.000	0.020	0.217	0.092	0.410	1.581	6.325
Benefits minus Costs	**-0.05**	**-0.06**	**0.59**	**2.58**	**4.74**	**19.26**	**80.81**

project. We identified almost 16,000 "telecommutable" jobs for this employer.

It is also informative to review the ratios between benefits and costs. Clearly, at the beginning of the project—during project planning, participant selection and training—there are no benefits, just costs. In the case illustrated here, more than a year elapsed between initiation of the planning phase and the start of participant selection. Once the participants begin telecommuting, however, the benefits begin to accumulate. At some point, if all goes well, monthly benefits begin to exceed costs. At some further point, the payback or break-even point, cumulative benefits equal and begin to exceed cumulative costs. That break-even point for this project was at about month 11 after the selection process began. Figure 8-8 shows the historical and anticipated results for the project. Note that the computer and software costs mentioned above are included as costs to the employer in this analysis, even though those costs were borne by the telecommuters.

Table 8-4 shows these results in numerical form. The drop in benefit-to-cost ratios in years 6 and 7 is a result of training and computer purchases for the large numbers of new telecommuters assumed in the model. If future experience matches the data derived thus far, the post-project benefit-to-cost ratios could regularly exceed 100 to 1, once all of the telecommuters are trained and computer purchases are completed! The average annual *net* benefit per telecommuter in this example project—and in similar ones for which I have data—is about $8,000.

This model assumes that only 40% of new telecommuters would receive employer-furnished computer equipment. This is felt to be conservative, since almost three-quarters of the telecommuters are now providing their own equipment. In a broader operational situation, those computer costs might be higher—or lower. Similarly, expansion of telecommuting to a broader selection of employees might result in lower effectiveness increases. In any case, the data at this point make it clear that telecommuting is working very well for this employer and is far above a simple break-even situation.

WHAT ABOUT US?

Employee

Most of the above discussion focuses on the employer. What about employee costs and benefits? Home-based telecommuters are the only ones with added monetary costs of telecommuting. These include: space in their homes that is reserved solely for telecommuting, and any added costs of office equipment and furniture, computers, software, telecommunications equipment, and telecommunications service charges that are not compensated by their employers.

In our sample case, home-based telecommuters, on average, used 170 square feet of their 1,850 square-foot homes; 130 square feet were reserved exclusively for telecommuting (the remainder also being used for other purposes). That is, the size of the dedicated office space at home, for which the employee pays the rent, taxes, and insurance, is about the same as, or larger than, the office space in the employer's facility. The most popular locations for the home office are a spare bedroom and the study or den, in that order. Note that in many countries, home sizes are roughly half that of the U.S. homes in our example. This does have an effect on the extent of home-based telecommuting in those countries.

There is generally no monetary compensation for this use of home office space, which I estimate has an annual cost (equivalent rental cost) of about $200. Employers typically do not reimburse their employees for the rental or related costs (except telephone); and, if they did, the Internal Revenue Service would probably count it as extra income since current IRS rules make it practically impossible to deduct home office space costs in tax returns.

Many employees already had office equipment and personal computers at home before they even heard about telecommuting. Almost exactly half of the applicants to large telecommuting projects in the late 1980s and early 1990s already owned personal computers. Of the remainder, about half stated that they would buy a computer if allowed to telecommute at least one day per week.

However, don't jump to the conclusion that the equipment investment is not a problem. Most of the telecommuters in these projects were mid-level employees, about two-thirds of them living in multi-earner households with household incomes significantly above the U.S. average. Some applicants were turned down because they needed a personal computer to telecommute and could not afford to buy it. This is why I used a value of 40% employer-purchased computers for new applicants to telecommuting projects. Employer purchases of portable computers—or even zero-interest purchase loans to employees—

can greatly expand the use of telecommuting to lower-income employees.

As explored earlier, I cannot find clear evidence of a net cost to telecommuters of utilities such as gas, electricity, and telephone. The differences seem to be buried in the inter-household variations in such costs. However, personal computers do use electrical energy, say, 1.6 kWh per day. Thus a computer-using, one-day-per-week telecommuter might incur added annual electricity costs (at $0.10 per kWh) of about $8.

The monetary benefits to telecommuters are generally in the form of reduced operating expenses: car use, clothing, food, and child care costs. The average telecommuter in the example case traveled 22.8 miles each way to work. Given an average automobile operating cost (including depreciation, fuel, insurance, and maintenance) of $0.42 per mile, the average one-day-per-week telecommuter saves about $920 per year.

I do not have accurate information on telecommuter savings in food and clothing. Typically, home-based telecommuters do not dress formally for their home office, nor do they eat out for lunch. My personal estimate is that the annual clothing bill is down by $200 for a one-day-per-week telecommuter, while lunch savings can amount to at least $2 per telecommuting day, or another $200 annually for one-day-per-week telecommuters.

Telecommuting is not a substitute for child or parent care; telecommuters can not work effectively and supervise other household members simultaneously. However, telecommuters may be able to hire lower-cost in-home supervisors for either small children or invalid relatives. I do not have estimates for these savings.

Because of the wide variation in home-telecommuting scenarios, I do not have a number for the net monetary impact of telecommuting on an individual telecommuter, except that it is probably a net benefit. The most significant benefit for home-telecommuters is psychological: stress reduction, feelings of greater control of one's life, and increased family interaction, as discussed earlier.

Telework center telecommuters can have most of the benefits just described, with fewer costs, particularly in equipment and housing. This is most apparent for neighborhood telework centers, which are almost at home. Regional centers, to the extent that they are relatively distant from employees' homes and have more formal office atmospheres, may have somewhat lower net telecommuter benefits. There is simply too little experience to date with either of these forms for us to reach quantitative conclusions.

The Community

In the case examined here, the primary motivation for the telecommuting project was a community cost problem: air pollution. The community, via its regulatory powers, decided to transfer that cost to the polluters, or the employers thereof, by means of fines imposed on those who did not meet or exceed minimum standards.

If the telecommuting were to be extended to all of the potential participants in the example project, there would be an annual reduction in air pollution of about 6 million pounds of carbon monoxide, 1.2 million pounds of unburned hydrocarbons, and about 400,000 pounds of nitrogen oxides. The impact on reducing traffic congestion is harder to determine, but eliminating about 3,000 cars from the downtown commute every day (just from this employer) would likely have a significant impact on traffic flow.

That, in turn, would reduce air pollution further. The reduced traffic flow, since it would also proportionately reduce roadway wear and tear, would diminish highway infrastructure costs. Further, if large numbers of organizations were to adopt telecommuting, the existing transportation infrastructure could serve adequately for many more years, even under conditions of increasing local population growth.

Telecommuters also appear to be more likely to participate in local activities, participating in local political and service groups more frequently. The telecommuters are less worn out from the daily commute and have more discretionary time. There may also be a depressing impact on the crime rate; as residential neighborhoods increase the numbers of people who are present during daylight hours, property crime and drug sales are likely to drop.

None of these community-impact speculations can be proven as of this writing. The population of telecommuters in the U.S., although several million strong, is too dispersed for the effects to show unequivocally.

Stick around, you'll see.

PART

2

FOR THE TELECOMMUTER

Preparing to Work at Home

There are two parts to getting started at home telecommuting. The first part is establishing your home office and setting up a good working environment. The second part is getting yourself together and rearranging your head so that it, too, works well in this new situation.

Setting up a Home Office

The first item on the agenda is defining the physical space where you are going to work. If you are already a multimillionaire, or otherwise have a 25,000 square foot cottage with detached office complex, this may not be an important consideration. Otherwise, here are some rules of thumb for finding that ideal location at home. For more information about the architectural details, you might want to consult a book on the topic.[1]

Locating the Workspace

The Best Choice

If you already have an office or den in a detached building, such as a converted garage or guest house, and the office has enough electrical power and environmental control (windows and/or air

---

[1] One example is *Home Offices & Workspaces*, by the editors of Sunset Books and Sunset Magazine. Lane Publishing Company, Menlo Park, CA., 1986.

conditioning and adequate lighting) to make working life comfortable, and if no one else in the family has the least desire to use that same space, then your search is over.

If you have a den, basement, attic, or spare bedroom of sufficient size that is not being used by anyone else, then you are in almost as good shape as the outside facilities owner. Sufficient size means at least as much space as you have in your present office away from home (you may still be thinking of that as your principal office). If you plan to use a personal computer or other technology as part of your work, make sure there is room for it and all of its or your accessories (printer, plotter, filing cabinet(s), reference works, books, fax machine, photocopier, answering machine, etc.). Figure at least 100 square feet for a permanent installation, more if you already have other things in there that can't be displaced. If you're going to use a computer or other electrical gadgets make sure that there is adequate electrical power. You may not need much but it's nice to have several outlets conveniently located.

Next Best

If there is no place at home that is sacrosanct, then there are two considerations to make. First, can you find a location in the house where you can still set up a permanent office layout, even though the room may also be used by others in the family? If so, this may work well, particularly if the other users of the space aren't there when you are.

Take a careful look around your home. There may be little used closets, alcoves or other nooks that, with a little ingenuity, can be turned into effective and permanent office space. There are two key selection criteria:

- The office should be out of the daily traffic flow of the rest of the family—that is, relatively out of sight.
- It should be relatively quiet, at least free from unwanted disturbances.[2]

If the space available just isn't large enough, you can resort to the use of fold up or stow-away furniture to compress the office at times when you are not using it. There are a number of commercially available desks geared for computer use that collapse into inscrutable small cabinets during leisure hours. In either case you will still need space around you while you are working. You may have to move the grand piano or the billiard table from the sitting room in order to do this, but it will be worth it in the long run.

Worst

Avoid using the kitchen, dining room table, bedroom or bathroom as a work place unless you're going to quit using it for its original purpose. Avoid temporary work places of all sorts, unless you plan to be only a very sporadic telecommuter, or you are the sole human inhabitant of your home.

Also avoid locating your office where it can easily be seen from outside the house or apartment or condo, particularly if you're a computer user and all that expensive equipment can be seen from outside. Burglars love it!

Face-to-Facing It

You should also consider how much contact you are going to have with business visitors. Business callers should find a clear, unobstructed route to the home office.[3] A separate outside door would be ideal. Other household members must find that they and their friends can still come and go freely without imposing on your home business environment.

In these cases, the living room, rather than your office space, may be the best location for meetings. The trick is to have the

---

[2] "Wanted" disturbances include such things as the doorbell and cries of distress from the kids.

[3] This can be an important factor in deciding whether a home-based telecommuter should have meetings at home. The primary issue is liability if a visitor is injured at/in a telecommuter's home. The question of responsibility for maintenance of an environment without unusual physical risk should be settled before telecommuting begins.

room easily convertible in appearance between its business and family functions. My own home "conference center" is either the living room or the dining area/table, depending on the number of visitors and the meeting purpose. There is the occasional frantic scurry to get all the newspapers, magazines and crockery stuffed away somewhere (typically on top of the washing machine) before the visitors arrive.

Inventorying Furniture

If you will be spending considerable amounts of time in front of a personal computer or some other "workstation", it is important that you have a setup that is comfortable and safe for you to work in. This often means that standard household furniture is not adequate for the job. What you need is a good desk, comfortable (long term) chair, accessible storage space, a place to put your printer and other accessories, and some effective area and/or task lights.

Especially important is the furniture with which you work. You should aim for minimizing fatigue and maximizing convenience. The furniture doesn't have to be "high tech" for it to be useful. Here are the key requirements, based on years of ergonomic research:

Seating Position

Regardless of any computer use, the main requirement is that you have a chair that lets you sit comfortably erect, with your thighs parallel to the floor or slightly up at the knees and your spine unslumped. That means the front of the seat should be slightly higher than the rear and the back of the chair should be tilted back somewhat (about fifteen degrees, according to ergonomists). Arm rests are OK if they don't get in the way of your desk or workstation activities. This works out (for the average-sized person) to a seat height of nineteen to twenty-one inches. An ergonomic secretarial chair is fine for this, but any other that fits the positioning requirements will do if it also has good lower back support. Many regular household chairs fail to meet these standards. Nice, comfortable arm chairs are deadly in this respect.

Desk Height

If you are working with a computer it is likely that a standard office desk will be too high. The key requirement here is that your forearms should be parallel to the floor and your wrists should be straight (unbent) when you are keying in information on the computer keyboard. You should also have space in front of the keyboard for the heels of your hands to rest while you are keying. For the average person this works out to a desktop height of about twenty-seven inches.

Display Position

If you are using a computer regularly, the center of its display screen should be about two feet from your face and about twenty degrees below the horizontal (about eight inches below eye level) for best comfort and ELF[4] safety. If you're a touch-typist and you do a lot of working from paper copy then you should have a device for holding the paper at about the same height, to minimize eye and neck/shoulder fatigue. If you're a hunt and peck typist you might want to have a copy holder set between the keyboard and the display.

Access to Telephone and/or Electrical Outlets

If you need to install a personal computer you may also need an extension cord or multi-outlet power block. But don't forget, an employer-sponsored home work environment must meet minimum standards to ensure safety of employer-owned equipment and of household members.

For those jobs requiring a computer, grounded electrical outlets are essential. Although newer residential construction

---

[4] Extremely Low Frequencies; the radiation emitted by many CRT (cathode ray tube) monitors in the range above about 50 Hz. Most very new monitors on the market conform to Swedish standards for radiation safety, so this is probably not a concern. Medical research on what constitutes a "safe" level of ELF is still underway.

will likely have the three-prong outlets, older homes may need to be wired for home telecommuting. Special surge protectors also may be desirable to protect the computer from "spikes" in the electrical power line. In areas where there are chronic, or even infrequent, brownouts or other power failures, consider adding an uninterruptible power supply (UPS) to the list of crucial equipment. All it takes is one or two power failures that would result in lost or damaged files to recoup the cost of the protection—not to mention the screaming and hair-tearing that tends to accompany such events.

An additional "work" telephone line will be necessary if you tele-access another computer frequently or for long periods during hours that a home phone is needed by other household members. Installation of a separate line will also be required for jobs involving a high volume of telephone calls to or from your home. Not all telecommuters need extra phone lines, however. In our experience,[5] about 30% of telecommuters have multiple telephone lines—as compared with about 20% multiple-line ownership by non-telecommuters.

To the degree that your work requires time-critical co-worker or other people contact, call forwarding, a telephone answering machine, voice or electronic mail—or a pager—will be required for efficient job performance.

The problem with many of the message storage systems is that they do not have a fail-safe method of notifying you that a message is waiting. This is particularly the case with electronic mail. The lack of a message-waiting message must be replaced by habit, a pager, or by a telecommunications software package that dials the mail center at fixed times(s) daily.

Noise Abatement

If you're going to work at home, you have to be protected from household noise—and the rest of the household has to be protected from your noise.

If you're a computer user, the most likely noise source is a printer. Think about that before setting up an office in the bedroom or anywhere that noise will disturb other family members. Printers are getting quieter every year but, unless you have a laser or ink-jet printer, they still make very discernible noise. Unlike the situation in many on-site environments, you

---

[5] These data are from studies by JALA of City of Los Angeles telecommuters over the period 1990 to 1992.

can insulate yourself by closed doors, background music, or other solutions to achieve the level of sound at which you work most productively.

If telephone contact is part of your job it is your responsibility to ensure, for example, that the family dog is not barking—or the vacuum cleaner is not running—next to the telephone. (Of course, this only happens during long distance or otherwise important calls.) It is your responsibility to be thoroughly professional to the degree that the work requires.

Acoustic isolation can get out of hand, however. One telecommuter was so concerned about being able to concentrate on her work that she firmly shut the door to her home office in order to eliminate any distracting noise. She finished about three days' worth of work on her first day of telecommuting. Yet, when she came in to her principal office the next day, expecting praise from her boss, she was astonished to discover that he had been trying to get her on the phone all day and, since she didn't answer—the phone being in the other room—was convinced that she was at the beach all day! He didn't bother to listen to her explanation. An instant casualty of insensitive management, she quit telecommuting. It took considerable persuasion to get their communication patterns back to the point where she could resume telecommuting.

Turf Struggles

If you already have a work space established at home, and the rest of the family *knows* it's your space, then you can skip this part. Otherwise it is important to select a work-place location that has the least intrusion on household space already used by other members of the family, consistent with the other requirements for your own working comfort. You may have to make some deals with other members of the family to get this to happen. But all parties involved should know whose space gets moved, and whence, before you start telecommuting. This need not be blown up to a U.N.-level negotiation, a short discussion with the interested parties may be sufficient.

And don't forget that your territorial incursions can be time-limited—that is, working hours only, if you have a sufficiently collapsible workstation. In multi-earner households, this is often not a problem—until it becomes a multi-telecommuter household!

Designing Your Workspace

Now, with all these thoughts in mind, become an instant architect. Get some graph paper with a square grid and lay out your proposed work space. Pick a scale; for example, 1 inch on the graph paper equals 1 foot in the house (¼ inch on the paper equals 3 inches in the real world). Make cutouts for all the pieces of furniture—and large equipment—you think you will need: desk, chair(s), table(s), telephone, modem, printer stand, exercise machine, file cabinet(s), bookshelves, lamps, whatever you feel is necessary. Lay out the walls, doors, and windows on the graph paper, including the swing space needed for doors (if any). Don't forget that you need room to walk in and to have access to drawers.

If you're using a computer and you get direct sunlight in the room, lightly draw in the angles of the incoming light rays. You'll want to avoid direct reflections from the computer display into your eyes. You'll also want to avoid reflections from well-lit walls behind you onto your display screen. Finally, you need to avoid having the screen between you and a bright area light source behind it. If you can't avoid these by workstation placement, be sure that you can screen off the offending light source when necessary. There are screens that you can buy to fit over the display screen and reduce glare, but these add costs and often are dust catchers. Many recent monitor screens have built-in glare-reduction features that further help reduce the problem.

You also may be able to adjust light levels with available lamps or drapes. Or supplementary lighting may be part of the equipment that you or the company should supply to achieve the proper work environment. Task lighting may be sufficient, and is generally preferable to area lighting.

Think of the activities you do most. Arrange the furniture so that whatever is required for those activities is within arm's reach—or a short roll of your chair.[6] Other, less-frequently used items can be placed farther away.

Try to arrange any electronic hardware so that:

- It is near electrical outlets and can be connected via a surge protector/master switch. If you live in an area that has frequent power fluctuations or outages, think about getting an Uninterruptible Power Supply (UPS) to prevent your screams of agony when the computer loses all of the stuff that you have been inputting but haven't bothered to save for the last two hours
- Interconnecting cables are out of the way, tied together, or covered to minimize the danger of tripping over them and to reduce the amount of dust they catch
- Heavy items are on secure stands, preferably near a wall, and as child-proofed as possible (even if the kids are only occasional visitors). If you live in earthquake country you may want to secure them to a wall or desk with a flexible cable. You may be able to use Velcro strips on the bottom of lighter objects.

If you're a smoker, remember that ashes and computers are bitter enemies, as are spilled coffee and floppy disks.

Keep the telephone ringer, or anything else with a magnet—like those nice little paper clip holders, away from floppy disks.

Keep frequently used manuals or other references on a shelf next to or above your computer display. Remember to put them back right after you've used them.

Add your own inspirations here:

_____

_____

_____

Securing Your Equipment, Materials, and Supplies

First, a fundamental point. Make sure you list the supplies you'll need at home *before* you embark on your telecommuting adventure. The list should include the obvious things, such as

---

[6] Don't try this if your chair doesn't have rollers on the legs!

paper and pencils, but keep an eye out for those not-so-obvious things: stapler, staple remover, phone number file, ruler, address or appointment book, calendar, manuals, and so on.

Particularly if you have children who love to play with mom's or dad's fascinating equipment, or who really need some of those supplies for school, it may be necessary to have a secure storage place for critical items. Paper and printer supplies can be in a cabinet that is locked or otherwise established as solely yours. (If you have a printer stand, the paper often can be kept in a box below it.) In any case it is your responsibility to ensure that your home office is a safe place to work in and that it is always in good shape for the work to be performed.

Computer Security

The computer can be kept in a desk or cabinet that is lockable. Floppy disks can be put in lockable (non-magnetic) storage bins. Many computers have lockable keyboards to foil the attempts of the kids to play with the machine while you're off somewhere else. Computer viruses are a growing worry; never boot your computer from a floppy disk unless you are sure it is an original or has an exact copy of the manufacturer's operating system software and boot tracks.[7]

Computer bulletin board systems (BBSes) are particularly worrisome, even nightmare-producing, to company computing executives. Publicly available BBSes are a favorite target for

---

[7] If you don't understand that sentence, check with your local computer guru.

hackers whose idea of entertainment is destroying someone else's data. Either don't connect to BBSes with your computer or, if you must try it, make very sure that any downloadable files of the BBS are well policed by its operator and/or that you habitually use a good brand of virus-protection software.[8]

Getting Down to Work

Training Yourself

Home is definitely not the office that you are used to. Working at home gives you great new freedoms. That's the trouble. You have to find that happy balance between the new freedoms and the responsibilities of getting the work out. That involves cultivating some self-discipline that you may not have needed in the office. Here are some pointers for keeping yourself working when you should be—and not working when you shouldn't be.

While I'm on the isolation question, someone who has supervised a telecommuting employee once observed, "the office environment has evolved for a reason." Going to work separates one from all but the most urgent non-work responsibilities. Establishing an office environment in the home is not only a physical problem but, more importantly, a conceptual task. The worker, household members and neighbors must be convinced that the telecommuter is at work. A three-year-old's demands for attention are difficult to ignore. Some double duty is a benefit of being at home: accepting a UPS delivery at the door is a more efficient use of time than driving to the depot. In effect, the home worker is substituting a new set of interruptions for some of those he has become accustomed to on site.

Some such interruptions require imaginative solutions. If a responsible relative is not available, it may be necessary to hire supplemental child care and insist that while Mommy or Daddy is "at work" she or he is not to be disturbed. This is particularly true for pre-school children. The neighbor will have to be "trained" not to drop in. With no hard and fast rules, the overriding guideline is that it is the worker's responsibility to improvise whatever adjustments are necessary for him or her to do the job on time and up to standard.

However, it is possible to set up a system of protocols for handling the most common sources of interruption listed above and provide training in dealing with them. Each protocol is of

---

[8] If you don't understand that sentence, check with your local computer guru.

the type: "In this situation . . . here are the steps to be taken to deal with the problem." This is described in Chapter 6.

Achieving the Office Frame of Mind

The first thing to settle is getting your mind to believe that you're in the office even though the evidence of your eyes and ears is that you're at home. That is one reason why it is important to establish a definite work space in the home that is clearly different from the rest of the space. The environment around your desk gives you the clues that it's an office. That extra easy chair may be tempting, but do you really work better while sitting in it?

The next important factor contributing to that frame of mind is the schedule. Set one up for every day that you're at home—and try to stick to it. That's the bad news. The good news is that it doesn't have to be the schedule you would use if you were actually in your principal office. It may overlap your ordinary schedule, particularly when you have to make phone or computer calls to others, to the public, clients or colleagues. But those times when such contact is unnecessary can be rearranged to suit your style. Many people stick to the regular office schedule anyway. Others work for a few hours early in the day, followed by some leisure time, then another stint in late afternoon and/or evening. Try a few of these options, after first discussing and agreeing upon them with your supervisor. But ultimately it is easiest if you get into a specific pattern of work hours that is consistent from day to day.

Clothes May Make a Difference

The first impulse of many telecommuters is to get away from office garb entirely; stick to jeans and sweatshirt, bathing suit, birthday suit, very informal wear. If it makes you feel more energetic, do it. Some telecommuters find that wearing more formal clothes helps keep them work-aware, even to the extent of wearing a suit in the home office. If you feel uncomfortable in casual clothes (or in a suit) change to the reverse.

Getting Organized

One of the hardest tasks at first may be sorting out what belongs where. I call it "The Two-Briefcase Syndrome." You may be familiar with it already. If you're at home the report you need to reference is in the old office. If you're in the old office the report you need is at home. So what do you do? You trudge back and forth between home- and old-office with two briefcases full of papers that you just might need.[9]

While this may be great for bodybuilding it is not an answer to your quest for serenity. Start keeping records on what is needed where. In some cases you can move non-sensitive files or references permanently home. In other cases you might want to have duplicates at home. In either case get into the habit of planning ahead of time what you'll need to have with you either at home or in the old office. The test of your success is when you graduate to a single—or no—briefcase.

Here's another trick. Think about what you do at home in terms of communicating and non-communicating time. Try to bunch the communicating time into coherent groups. That is, try to make all your phone calls (or return calls), fax transmissions, etc., in a specific time interval. This way, you can increase the amount of uninterrupted time you have. That, in turn tends to both increase your effectiveness and decrease your stress levels.

Many telecommuters notice a positive side-effect of this. They become generally better organized. They plan more carefully, visualizing exactly what's needed for the next step, the next job. This carries over into tasks that have nothing to do with telecommuting.

"Leaving" the Office

Sometimes it's harder to leave the office at home than it is to leave the distant one. "Just one more calculation (or paragraph) and I'll quit for sure, dear." One of the prime dangers for happy telecommuters is workaholism. As in the case of getting in the frame of mind to do work at home, you may want to set up a schedule of sacrosanct non-work hours.

Some telecommuters have gone to the extent of having an outside door installed in the room they use as an office. In the morning they go out of the front door of the house (or apartment if they have an understanding landlord) and go in the new office door, reversing the trip at day's end.

---

[9] One telecommuter had a trunk full of files in the car—just in case.

Then, of course, there's the topic of brief visits. Sometimes you have really brilliant work-related ideas during non-working hours. Should you try to remember them until the next work period or rush right into your home office and get them into action? Our experience is to do the latter; it is much more satisfying and quite possibly takes less time than if you try to remember it all later.

We also advise you to keep going on those occasions when you're really on a roll; get those great ideas down even if you are working past your schedule—just don't make a habit of it.

Our experience also shows that working at home is more intense than working in the traditional office. You tend to get much more done in a given amount of time, provided that it is the kind of work suited for a home office. Make use of that intensity in scheduling your hours, both in and out of the office. Work when you feel that you can best exert that intensity; do something else when you feel a need for change. But keep in mind that the measure of success in this new work environment is output.[10]

Exercise

Working from home also gives you a chance to get that exercise that you never had time for when you had to commute every day. Make pushing yourself away from the refrigerator one of your first daily routines. One telecommuter gets up in the morning and goes straight to the home office for an hour or so. Then this telecommuter runs or goes swimming, comes back for a shower and breakfast, then it's back to the home office. The exercise time also turns out to be useful for arranging or re-examining the thoughts from the earlier work session. Both the thoughts and the telecommuter end up in better shape.

If you're a constant computer user it's also a very good idea to take regular breaks[11] to walk around, water the plants or the pets, or otherwise loosen up from the time you've spent in a fixed position at the keyboard. There are even exercise books for the office-bound.

---

[10] This doesn't mean that you should feel free to reduce the length of your work day. After all, telecommuting does cost extra and your increased productivity is one of the ways of compensating for those costs.

[11] About 15 minutes every hour for constant computer users; about 15 minutes every two hours for intermittent computer users.

Training the Household

You are not the only one who has to get in shape for working at home. Removing the distractions of home can be a—or *the*—major task in setting up a good working environment. The hardest part is usually training the rest of the family that when you are working you are working and are not to be disturbed any more than you would be if you were in the principal office. You are not available for running down to the store for groceries. You are not available for random questions and interruption from the spouse and kids. You are working.

Noise

As I mentioned earlier, one of the common distractions is background noise while you are on the phone. Vacuum cleaners, washing machines, crying children, barking dogs and parrots with colorful vocabularies make poor impressions of businesslike behavior to the party on the other end of the line. The best solution is to have your home office in a room where you can shut the door and isolate those noises. Failing that, if there is someone else at home to take care of the noise sources, make sure that that person takes care of the problem promptly.

On the other hand, if you miss some of the office sounds, fear not. Tapes are available of typewriters clacking, copiers copying, water coolers glukking, and other office environmenta.

Toddler Tension

The subject of noise brings up the issue of telecommuters with young children. Contrary to one's initial hopes, it is not a great idea to try to telecommute and personally take care of an active three-year-old simultaneously. Although it can be done, and is more satisfying than leaving the job to a sitter, it is much better to try to arrange the schedule so that you are working while the child is asleep or is being supervised by some other responsible person. In the latter case, this may also take some training of the prospective sitter.

This does not mean that you can't telecommute if you're a single parent, or have pre-school kids or invalid parents. It does mean that there should be someone else present in the household who can handle the non-emergency, routine care of those dependents while you're working. You're still available for the occasional crisis.

Diplomacy

You are not a flaming tyrant, we hope. The best policy seems to be to get the family together before you start working at home, explain the situation carefully, then reinforce the rules, gently, as such situations arise when you are actually working at home. Many telecommuters have found that everything settles down after a few weeks. The kids or spouses no longer disturb them, but still feel better for having the parents around even though they are nominally not available.

Keep the assertiveness image in mind, though. One of the advantages of working at home is that you are available for those really special occasions—or emergencies—that come up from time to time. Firmness combined with flexibility is the key.

One telecommuter did have an unusual problem, though. His dog loved having him home; got so accustomed to it that, when he did go to the principal office once or twice a week, the dog was inconsolable and howled all day. This did nothing to improve relationships with the neighbors. What would you do in that situation?[12]

Dealing with the Neighbors and Drop-in Traffic

Speaking of neighbors, they can present a few challenges. The first is convincing them that you really are working, not loafing or unemployed. It might help to have a little home-office-warming party to demonstrate your new operation.

That party might also be a good time to mention that you are not available as a baby sitter, parcel drop-off point, message taker, or coffee klatscher while you are working. This, too, might take a little polite reinforcing during the first few weeks of your new lifestyle. That doesn't mean that you can't have lunch with the neighbors or go out for short shopping tours, provided that these fit into your new schedule. One of the greatest appeals of telecommuting is that you can arrange many of these previously impossible conflicts in your newly flexible schedule.

In Japan the social mores about having a respectable job are particularly intense. I heard, but cannot verify, the following story: This social status situation quickly became painful to some Japanese telecommuters whose neighbors were completely unconvinced by explanations that they really hadn't lost their jobs (and major status). Their employer not only came to their

---

[12] Our solution: Get another dog to keep the first one company. It worked.

rescue but materially increased their status by sending around a company cleaning squad, complete with uniforms bearing the company logo, to the telecommuters' homes once a month!

Living Above What You Can't Change

Try as you might, some of the distractions and interruptions of working at home are unavoidable. You also must try to adapt yourself to those as well. Don't forget, there are many unavoidable distractions and interruptions in the traditional office as well. You may not be able to isolate yourself visually or acoustically from the other doings at home. If you can't arrange the schedule so that you miss particularly busy periods, try some mental conditioning (or local background music) so that you learn to ignore the distractions. It does work. On the other hand, don't get so isolated that you miss important calls, such as those from the boss!

Also, don't get frustrated if not everything works well at first. We routinely find that new telecommuters need a few weeks to make adjustments and get the work patterns smoothly developed. Your attitude is really important during that time. Use your ingenuity to get around obstacles that may come up. We have yet to find a difficulty that can't be surmounted by some careful planning or attitude adjustments on your—or your supervisor's—part.

10 Telecommuting Management

Meanwhile, Back On Site

Successful management *of* telecommuters is another key topic, and is covered in earlier chapters. Here we cover successful management *by* telecommuters: the aspects of telecommuting management that are important for you to understand as a telecommuter who is being supervised by a telemanager.

New Working Relationships with Co-workers

One of the worries of new telecommuters is that they will lose contact with their fellow workers, that they somehow will become different in the eyes of their colleagues. This fear is sometimes abetted by the treatment they get when they do come into the office, sort of a new form of hazing. "Oh, I see you've finally decided to come in to work for a while!" "Well, stranger, how was the vacation?" "Didn't you used to work here?" These and similar remarks are not too successful in easing your tensions.

A related problem is the: "Gee, I hate to call you at home, but . . . ." The hidden meaning: You are somehow different (and worse, or luckier, or otherwise less understood) than everyone else. So here, as well as at home, there is some training and adjustment needed.

The first rule is: *Be positive, not defensive, about telecommuting*. Admit that you've been having a great time at home and, by the way, turned out that big report a week ahead of schedule and with much better insight than you could with all the interruptions at the office. Mention that you can now exercise regularly with no problems, now that you don't have to waste an hour or two on the road every day. Tell about the time you went sailing last Wednesday afternoon, having finished your work at home by 10:30 that morning. Or the play that your ten-year-old starred in that you went to see at her school. Or the town council seat that you're running for now that you have the time and energy to go to meetings. You get the idea. Just don't be obnoxious about it. On second thought, maybe you should keep some of those things to yourself. Just smile; make them wonder what you've been up to.

The second rule is: *Business as usual*. Make sure that your colleagues know that they can call you at home any time they would normally try to contact you at the office. One technique, probably a good one in any case if you have lots of phone traffic, is to have a separate phone line that is solely for business purposes. Give that number out to people. Print it on your business card.

Have call forwarding (together with an answering machine at home) or voice mail installed in the principal office so that calls get to you as expeditiously as possible. The trick here, as mentioned earlier, is to balance communications with uninterrupted think-work. To keep the interruptions down, the best trick may be to use a pager. If the people at the principal office really need you, you get beeped. Otherwise, you pick up the recorded communications in accordance with your[1] schedule, not the callers'.

Many people, particularly those not in your immediate office group, won't even know you're working from home. Make a particular effort to keep in frequent touch with your close colleagues via telephone, fax, or electronic mail (if you have the equipment or software). Don't wait for them to call you, call them. Try calling first thing in the morning a few times—before they've made it through the traffic. Or just before quitting time—after they've left to catch the car pool; they'll get the message.

---

[1] This advice is given on the assumption that your primary job requirement is other than immediately responding to external calls.

The real secret to breaking down those misunderstandings is frequent communication. What we're doing in telecommuting is substituting some telecommunication for face-to-face conversation. We do not eliminate communication. Nor do we eliminate face-to-face conversation. We may actually increase the amount of total communication by this new combination. But it may take some real effort on your part to keep the communication going.

Which brings us to rule three: *Go to the principal office regularly to reinforce your telecommunications.*

"Regularly" can mean anything from a few days a year to four days per week, depending on all those other job factors we covered earlier. For the average contemporary telecommuter, it means about three days per week. One of the important parts of this rule is that you may have to schedule meetings more tightly, and make sure that the meetings you do have are short and to the point. This tactic allows you to move your meetings into as few days as possible. (This in itself is a productivity enhancer.)

Many telecommuters find that they can set agendas for the meetings and transmit the necessary background material to the attendees by electronic mail and telephone or facsimile from home (or via a secretary who just might be at home). They also find that this preparation significantly shrinks meeting time. In some cases, you can attend the meetings electronically, via telephone[2] or video teleconferencing.

Try to have at least one day per week when you are always at home. This helps get you, your family, and your colleagues acclimated to telecommuting. Of course, this is not always possible; occasional crises do seem to intervene, but it is a good idea to try. In a matter of a few weeks to a few months your telecommuting will be routine to all concerned.

Job (Re)design

Sometimes it seems that, no matter how you try, you can't arrange your schedule—or the schedules of others—so that you can telecommute effectively. Maybe this situation calls for some rethinking of the content of your job and the jobs of your co-workers. For example, one telecommuter was responsible for

---

[2] The Telecommuting Advisory Council, Inc. (TAC), is a non-profit educational organization dedicated to disseminating information about telecommuting. TAC holds periodic telephone teleconferences to report on the status of telecommuting activities and discuss telecommuting-related issues. Participation in the teleconferences is limited to people on Earth, so far.

certifying that new test equipment shipped to her organization was operating properly. The rules of her job also required that the certification be made within twenty-four hours of the equipment's arrival. Unfortunately, the equipment never arrived according to a preset schedule; often it appeared when she was telecommuting from home. She began missing those twenty-four-hour deadlines, her co-workers were getting upset because they couldn't handle the inspections. Her supervisor, uneasy about telecommuting from the start, was preparing to stop it all.

What should be done? One possibility is for the telecommuter's job to be redesigned to share inspection responsibility among two or three of her co-workers. This is usually known as *cross-training*. Each is responsible for equipment inspection on the specific days when he or she is in the principal office. This has extra benefits: co-workers who could not telecommute before (because of similar job restrictions) are free to telecommute; job responsibilities and knowledge are expanded for all concerned.

In a situation like this the important first step is to look at your entire work group as a collection of tasks to be performed. See how reallocation of those tasks among the existing workers can free up more people's time for telecommuting. Don't forget, if you want someone else to take over some of your responsibilities then you have to take over some of the other person's in return.

The buddy system is a variation of this. Many telecommuters keep a file cabinet in the principal office with copies of the current "hot" project materials in them, together with an easily identified index of what's where. When the inevitable crisis comes and the boss wants to know *now* about project X, your designated buddy in the office can retrieve the key material, after a phone call to you. The crisis gets solved without the necessity of your coming to the office.[3] As in the previous case, make sure that you return the favor for your buddy.

Communicating with Your Supervisor

What nags at managers' nerves the most is the thought that you really might be out playing instead of working! This is exacerbated when the manager calls you in mid-day and you

---

[3] This doesn't always work; some crises really *will* require your in-person attendance. Be willing to make those appearances cheerfully.

really are out playing golf—even though you got up at 4:00 A.M. to get the day's work out of the way first.

Quality communication with your supervisor can be even more important, at least to your career plans, than communication with others. One of the central management issues of telecommuting is the shift from focusing on how many hours you put in to something that is more performance-oriented.

Attitudes are crucial here. The real secret of successful telecommuting rests on *mutual trust* being established between you and your supervisor. If your supervisor already trusts you to deliver the goods regardless of whether you are at home or in the office, and if you trust your supervisor to reward you justly for work well done, then that is all you need. If you have established this bond of mutual trust and respect you can work anywhere that is feasible within the other constraints of the job.

If some of this is missing on one or both sides, or even if you are a little uncertain about this new venture, it may be worth getting a little more formal about telecommuting. What seems to work best for telecommuters is almost a contractual relationship between you and your supervisor. You jointly have to agree on the following:

- what is the product—what *specifically* it is that you are supposed to do
- what resources you will need to do it
- when it is supposed to be finished
- how you recognize the finished product (and, for long duration projects, the intermediate stage products)
- quality or success criteria for the results

. . . just as if you were an independent consultant hired by the Company.

If possible, get the main points of your mutual understanding in writing, although it need not be nearly as complex or intimidating as a formal contract. Then be sure that you fulfill your end of the bargain. As you start telecommuting, it is particularly important to build up your supervisor's confidence (and possibly your own) that you can do the work well, and on time, even though you're not always in the office.

Part of the task of setting up that first understanding is agreeing on performance standards. If you have a very well-defined job, and it is perfectly clear to both you and your supervisor what it is that you are supposed to do, this is easy. The less well-defined your job is, or the more subject it is to sudden changes in direction, the harder it is to nail down the performance criteria—and the more important it is to arrive at a joint understanding of what it is that you are supposed to do, and how well you are to do it. Try to work out a description anyway, as well as the two of you can. Then reexamine it at appropriate intervals to ultimately fine-tune it or, better yet, find out that you don't really need it at all.

The length of the interval for reexamination also depends on your job. Think of the tasks you do in your job. How long does it take to do the longest duration task? Hours? Days? Weeks? Months? If it's one of the last three, pick an interval about one-fourth of that for your initial performance reviews. As your mutual confidence grows, the interval between reviews may also. Don't forget, the boss may be a telecommuter too.

An example of a written understanding is in Appendix B.

Feedback and Help

One of the first worries about home telecommuting is that you're alone out there! What happens when things go wrong?

Technical Problems for Computer Users

This may be particularly important if your telecommuting involves intensive use of a computer and you are new to the foibles of the machines. Microcomputers do break, although it is fairly infrequent. More often they do inexplicable things—like becoming suddenly catatonic—that are nerve-wracking even in the office where there may be ready help at hand. At home such ill-mannered machines can be even more threatening. What to do?

First, don't be afraid to ask "dumb" questions, either over the phone or in person when you are in the principal office. If you don't completely understand how something works, or can be fixed, ask. If your machine suddenly seems to die, before you do anything else ask someone how to fix it. (Remember Murphy's Law, Corollary 53: The machine will usually die just before the report is due and you have worked the last seven and a half hours without once saving your data on a disk.) Dumb questions are not at all dumb if they save you later grief. We know of many pairs of telecommuters who have solved equipment and software problems over the telephone. This can work very well indeed. In fact, one of the things we would like you to do is jot down the technical problems you have had, or are having, so that the Company can come up with a more extensive "how to" for future telecommuters.

Meanwhile, the Company may have established a guru service for your hardware, software, and other technical questions. Check this out. If so, write down the particulars here, so you can find it later.

Your local guru's name is _____ .

Your guru can be reached at _____-_____ .

If you have problems, contact the guru first. However, you should also write down the solution or recovery process for each problem you run into. Keep those notes in an easily accessible place (your memory?) so you won't have to bother the guru with incessant repeat performances.

The Company should also have a series of workshops and other available types of training to help get you off to a roaring start as a computer telecommuter. Information on these training sessions can be obtained from _____ .

Physical Support

Despite all the forecasts to the contrary, the "paperless office" seems to be a long way off. Mail, supplies and materials still have to travel to and from your desk, wherever that desk is. If it is at home, the interoffice mail system won't reach. There are some ways to meet this problem. First, change the address on periodicals so that they come to your home instead of the office. Second, if you telecommute extensively arrange with a co-worker to drop off and pick up your interoffice mail daily or at appropriate intervals. Third, when you do go into the principal office pick up your mail and that of other nearby telecommuters; it still beats a car pool. Finally, try to convert most of your interoffice messaging to electronic mail, voice mail, facsimile, or telephone conversations.

Some equipment problems and repairs just can't be done easily at home. They require that the offending box be taken somewhere for surgery. As the background information says, sometimes you may have to go into the principal office until the offending machine is repaired or replaced.

Dealing with Personal and Household Compulsions and Relationships

There are problems and issues that a book this general in nature can not handle. For down-to-earth advice on how to deal with problems of overeating (the telecommuting refrigerator syndrome), kids or mates who can't seem to fit themselves into your new role (or vice versa), technical problems that the guru can't handle effectively, and similar problems, there seems to be no substitute for advice from others who have been through it. To that end, the Company should have periodic group sessions to explore problems and solutions offered by fellow telecommuters.

For issues that have to do with management or organizational problems, the best approach is to see your supervisor.

Dealing with the IRS

This is not a source of legal advice on the tax laws. You should consult your accountant for the latest information. However, current tax law makes it *very* difficult for you to have any tax advantage from an office at home.

Bailing Out

Sometimes, in spite of all our good intentions, you or your supervisor feel that telecommuting just isn't working out for you. If attempts to resolve the problems are not successful then the best solution seems to be to quit telecommuting from home. All that is necessary is that you tell your supervisor that you want to quit the project and you can arrange to return with no questions asked. This project is for volunteers and that commitment works both ways: you do not have to telecommute if you don't want to; similarly, your supervisor can ask you to stop telecommuting at any time. So, if you enjoy telecommuting, keep in mind the fact that telecommuting has to work for everyone concerned if it is to work at all.

Best wishes.

Appendix A:

Supervisor's Telecommuting Check List

To ensure that your telecommuting employee is properly acclimated to the Company Telecommuting Demonstration Project, the following checklist has been provided to you to follow during the orientation process. Employees who work only from telework center offices need not comply with items 4 and 6:

Subject   *Date Reviewed*

1. The employee has read and understood the explanatory materials in the TeleGuide.   _____

2. The employee has reviewed and signed the Telecommuter's Agreement form prior to actual participation in the project.   _____

3. The employee has been provided with a schedule of his or her work hours or guidelines for work hours. Consistent with Division rules and bargaining union contracts, all requests for overtime to be worked or use of sick leave, vacation, compensatory time off, or any other type of leave, must be approved in advance by the supervisor.   _____

4. Employee has been issued equipment as listed in the attached Exhibit A. (Note: To be included as appropriate.)   _____

5. Performance expectations were reviewed and jointly agreed upon.   _____

6. The employee is familiar with minimum requirements for safe and adequate office space at home and asserts that they have been met.   _____

I have reviewed the above listed items with _____ prior to his

Please Print

or her participation in the Telecommuting Demonstration Project.

_____   _____
Date   *Supervisor*

179

Appendix B:

- . - . - . - . -

Telecommuter's Agreement

In order to determine where and how telecommuting is a viable work alternative for the Company it is critical that specific data be collected from the participants in the Company Telecommuting Demonstration Project.

I understand that as a condition of my participating in the Company Telecommuting Demonstration Project I am responsible for providing the project leader with certain information discussed below. I further understand that my failure to provide this data within the specified time frames could result in my being removed from the project and returned to my former working status.

I also understand that I am required to adhere to the guidelines set forth in the *TeleGuide* and specifically to the following requirements. If I fail to do this my participation in the project will be withdrawn.

1. If I telecommute from home I am expected to keep my home telecommuting office as clean and free from obstructions as if it were my primary Company office. If I have a work-related accident at home, I am expected to report it promptly as if the accident had occurred in my primary Company office. If a third party is injured at my home in connection with my telecommuting work, I will report the accident and/or injury promptly to my supervisor.

2. It is my responsibility to ensure that any Company equipment and software used in my job are used in businesslike conditions, whether at home or in a telework center. This includes protecting the Company equipment and software against abuse or other violation of existing Company rules concerning protection of its property. I may *not* use Company equipment or software for purposes in contradiction to Company, city, state, or federal laws, rules and/or regulations, or copyrights, nor may I or my family or friends use Company equipment or software to perform work for other employers.

3. Upon the receipt of authorization, I may use my own equipment and/or software to telecommute. Company assumes no responsibility for the maintenance or repair of my own equipment or software.

4. If there are any equipment or software failures while I am working at home, I am responsible for immediately informing my supervisor. I also understand that I may be asked to return to the primary office until repairs are completed or a substitute

has been provided. I further understand that any repairs made by the Company will be performed at a location designated by the Company.

5.   I will protect Company information and data against loss or misuse in accordance with all applicable Company rules and regulations, and with at least the same level of care as is used in the primary office.

6.   I understand that I will not get travel expenses for the times when I have to come in to my primary Company office for meetings. Mileage and per diem for work-related travel will be calculated from the primary Company office, home telecommuting office, or telework telecommuting office, as determined under existing guidelines.

7.   I must *average* at least one *full* day per week telecommuting over a six-month period to remain in the project.

8.   My specific telecommuting work periods will be arranged with my supervisor and may be revised at intervals throughout the project. All other work rules and approvals are as already established and remain in effect.

9.   At times during the course of the project I will be asked to complete a questionnaire covering work and telecommuting-related activities. These times will be: once near the beginning of telecommuting; once near the midpoint of the project; and once near the end of the formal part of the project.

Only the research team consisting of the Project Leader and those individuals conducting the project evaluation will have access to the detailed individual telecommuters' questionnaire and survey results. Company management participating in the project will have access to the statistical results and will, of course, be the ultimate decision makers for individual changes during the course of the project. All sensitive information will be kept strictly confidential; only aggregate results of the demonstration project will be released to anyone.

[The following paragraphs are for cases where the company wants to get detailed information on the effects of the telecommuting.]

10. I will participate in a three-day logging session of my, and my family's, daily car use. [This provision is for cases where the company needs to demonstrate reductions in car use.]

11. I will keep a monthly log of my utility bills (gas, telephone, and electricity) if I telecommute from home. [This provision is for cases where the company wishes to identify the energy costs of telecommuting.]

12. I am to report any problems I may be having with—or because of—telecommuting to my supervisor (such as relatives or friends always popping in and causing distractions from work, feeling isolated and needing more interaction with my co-workers, etc.). I will also participate in occasional discussion group sessions for resolving these or other telecommuting-related problems.

13. If I have any questions regarding any of the above or regarding telecommuting, I will check with my supervisor.

I have read the TeleGuide and this document. I understand and accept the responsibility of adhering to the conditions set out above and in the TeleGuide and to providing the above listed information as a condition of participation in the Company Telecommuting Demonstration Project. I further understand that if I fail to adhere to these conditions my participation in the project may be withdrawn. I understand that changes in assignment may cause my removal from the project. I understand that I may be removed from the project at any time at the discretion of my supervisor.

_____   _____

Employee Signature   *Date*

_____

Supervisor Signature

Appendix C:

Department Telecommuting Policies

The following items governing telecommuting are to be filled in by your own department.

Equipment

In this section should be a list of the specific equipment provided either by the employee or by the Company in order for the employee to telecommute from home. The list should include, but not be limited to, personal computers, computer terminals, modems, printers, facsimile machines, typewriters, photocopy machines, and furniture.

Employee Responsibilities

This covers any general, department-specific responsibilities of telecommuters for care and handling of equipment, including any requirements for insurance coverage.

Equipment and/or Software Installation

The Company is willing to install equipment in telecommuters' homes, or to subcontract such services. The costs will be billed to the user department. Each department should decide whether to use these services, provide its own, or leave any equipment installation to the ingenuity of the telecommuters. A similar situation prevails with software and the information services department.

Equipment Maintenance and Repair

In general, departments are expected to maintain and repair their own equipment and software, regardless of its location. However, policies may differ as to who should provide maintenance and repair of telecommuter-owned software and equipment that is used for Company business. The department's policy should be stated here.

Work Rules   This includes any department-specific rules on work hours
                                  and/or availability periods, meeting attendance, reporting
                                  schedules, and the like. It does *not* include the details of the
                                  employee's job requirements. That is covered in the *Detailed
                                  Work Agreement*.

Returning to Work   This covers any department-specific rules for termination of
                                  telecommuting.

Appendix D:

Detailed Work Agreement

This is to include any detailed agreements arrived at by you as the supervisor and your telecommuting employees during, or subsequent to, the joint telecommuting training session. The period covered, to be filled in above, is whatever is comfortable for both of you. It can range from a day or two to several months, depending on the level of autonomy to be assigned to the telecommuter.

Performance Evaluation Criteria

What objective[1] criteria are there, such as number and quality of reports completed, documents reviewed, audits performed, contacts made, lines of bug-free computer code produced, transactions processed, etc. In this section just list what they are. Don't get hung up on numerical criteria if they are not appropriate to the job.

Specific Work Objectives and Milestones

For example, in developing a plan the objectives might be: contacting or meeting with the key people affected by the plan; outlining its contents; developing agreement on the issues; suggesting and selecting approaches; developing consensus on the optimal approaches; drafting the plan; coordinating review of the draft; developing the final plan.

Milestones might be: meetings concluded; outline produced; first draft completed; final plan produced; each with an associated date.

Activities to Be Performed

This is a list of the specific activities that must be performed to meet the objectives above. It can be as terse or as prolix as you and your employee wish.

---

[1] The difficulty, of course, is in deciding what's objective and what's subjective, particularly where issues of quality are concerned. What is most important at this point is that both supervisor and supervisee agree on whatever the criteria are.

Anticipated Results   What are the end products of all this? In the example given it's a plan plus a state of mind (consensus, motivation) of the participants.

Index